A
Survival Guide
for
Project
Managers

A
Survival Guide
for
Project
Managers

James Taylor

AMACOM
American Management Association

New York • Atlanta • Boston • Chicago • Kansas City • San Francisco • Washington, D.C.
Brussels • Mexico City • Tokyo • Toronto

Library of Congress Cataloging-in-Publication Data

Taylor, James
    A Survival Guide for Project Managers / James Taylor.
       p.   cm.
    Includes bibliographical references and index.
    ISBN 0-8144-0337-9
    1. Industrial project management.   I. Title.
    HD69.P75T39   1998
    658.4'04—dc21   97–35492
                                                  CIP

Printing number

10   9   8   7   6   5   4   3   2

To Karen Romano-Taylor, my wife and best friend,
who makes everything in life worthwhile.

To my Mother, Clyde Martin,
who is certainly the best project manager I ever knew.

To my children,
Aimee Romano, Darcy Romano, and Michael Taylor,
the most successful and happiest projects I ever was
involved with.

And to my son, Paul Taylor,
a project in progress.

I love you all!

Contents

Acknowledgments

This book is the product of many years spent in learning to manage projects and organizations, and in teaching others what *I* have learned. To single out all the individuals who have shaped my thinking and learning, thereby contributing to whatever success I have achieved, would be impossible. There are a few, though, who *have* to be mentioned: Dr. Thomas Myerchin, who, as a teacher, colleague, and friend, instills the desire to learn more, do better, and always make a difference; Jerry Huguley, my lifelong friend and an outstanding project manager in his own right; and Mike Castronis, a man who had a major, positive impact on Huguley, me, and everyone else his life touched. I would be remiss if I didn't acknowledge that my continuing learning comes from teaching the inquisitive and bright students at Marymount University, Arlington, Virginia, and George Washington University, Washington, D.C. They require that my knowledge be current and the information I impart be usable.

I also want to express my gratitude to Tony Vlamis and his outstanding Editorial Assistant, Desirée Rivera, for their tireless help, professionalism, and good humor. They made writing a book a lot more fun than such an undertaking generally is.

Part One
Human Skills and Technical Tools

Introduction to Part One

Project management is a specialized approach to managing business, yet most project managers have never had any training, other than on-the-job training, about the art and science of project management. So mistakes are perpetuated, and a concept that came into being specifically to solve the problems of inefficient management itself becomes just another inefficient management concept.

This book is intended to provide new project managers and project team members with a fundamental understanding of project management essentials. These essentials are explained and discussed in Part One. Part Two discusses the phases of a project's life and how and when to apply the skill sets presented in Part One. With a solid base of knowledge about the technical and human tools of project management and when and how to use them, you can then confidently manage a project to successful conclusion.

What Is Project Management?

Project management is the art and science of managing relatively short-term efforts, having finite beginning and ending points, usually with a specific budget, and with customer-specified performance criteria. "Short term" in the context of project duration is dependent on the industry. For example, in the construction industry, a house might be built in three months, while a hospital might take two years. In the aerospace industry, a new airplane might take eight to ten years to design and build. In the Department of Defense's training environment, it is usual practice to award a contract for fifteen years for a contractor to manage, operate, and maintain a training complex. The longer and more complex a project is, the more it will benefit from the application of project management tools.

The concept of project management is relatively new. In the 1950s a conscious effort was made to devise specialized tools for managing the complex weapons systems being built for the Department of Defense. These tools are in widespread use today in all industries, public and private. The tools of project management make it a science. However, there is much more to managing projects than just applying analytical tools to help monitor, track and control them. The bigger problems for project managers are those associated with the human element: conflict resolution, team building, and negotiating. The application of the skills necessary to cope with this element constitutes the art part of project management.

Why Project Management?

The last forty years have witnessed a rapid and staggering change in technology and global competition. With these changes, the nature of business has become more complex and more dynamic. Companies have become more diverse in the products or services they offer, and increasing, or even maintaining, market share has become more competitive. In his book on project management, Harold Kerzner lists five questions:[1]

1. Are the projects technically complex?
2. Are there dynamic and stringent environmental or regulatory considerations?
3. Are the budget and schedule constraints tight?
4. Are there several tasks to be integrated?
5. Are there several functional boundaries to be crossed?

If the answer to any of these questions is yes, there may be a need for some form of formalized project management. When a company decides to approach its business from a project management perspective, the project manager is going to need two distinct classes of skills: technical, which deal with monitoring, tracking, and controlling a project, and interpersonal, which deal with the problems that invariably arise from the interaction of people with the project.

Technical Skill Requirements

Project managers do not have to be specialists in the project's technology. Some authorities indeed argue that project managers should be generalists because they thus have a better chance of understanding the project from a holistic point of reference. The more complex a project is—that is, the more subsystems to be integrated, the more tasks to be accomplished, and the more technically challenging the components—the better suited a generalist will be as the project manager. Regardless of the project manager's level of technical expertise, this person must have a good understanding of and facility in using several tools designed specifically for monitoring, tracking, and controlling the project. These tools are explained in Part One.

The increase in global competition and the extraordinary growth in information technology have created other problems for project managers—problems that have more to do with human relations than with technical skills.

Management Skill Requirements

There is much more demand on the project manager's interpersonal and negotiating skills today than even just fifteen years ago. The traditional, vertical organizational hierarchy, which was the model for all organizational structures since it was invented by the early Roman army until the mid-1900s, is too slow and inflexible to respond to today's competitive challenges, and information technology is being used, among other things, to disperse the workforce from centralized and expensive office complexes to smaller telecommuting sites or home offices.

Other attempts to cut costs include the establishment of

cross-functional teams to use the resources of the company better, flattening the organization to reduce management levels and expedite decision making and communication, and using fewer but better-trained people.

All of these efforts at making the company more efficient and cost-effective are precisely the areas that project management was developed to handle. But with the relatively recent emphasis on cross-functional teams, flat organizational structures, increasing diversity in the employee ranks, and empowerment of employees, project managers have to be more than just technical managers; they have to be team builders and negotiators as well. These and other skills are discussed in Part One.

It is important to understand the technical and management tools needed for project management, but without the knowledge of when and how to apply them, the skills are useless. In Part Two, we explore the phases of a project's life cycle and demonstrate how the tools are applied in each of the phases.

This brings us to the objective of this book: to provide a balance between the technical and management skills required and the knowledge of how and when to apply them.

This book is written to be consistent with the standards and principles of the Project Management Institute (PMI) and the Project Management Book of Knowlege (PMBOK). PMI and PMBOK are discussed in Chapter 1 in the discussion on project management skills and the problems of project management.

Note

1. Harold Kerzner, *Project Management: A Systems Approach to Planning, Scheduling, and Controlling*, 5th ed. (New York: Van Nostrand Reinhold, 1995).

Section I: The Human Skills

Chapter 1
Project Management Skills

Today, inspiration, though still necessary, is no longer enough for the manager.
—Peter Guest, *How to Manage Large Multidisciplinary Engineering Groups*

Managing projects in today's environment of large, complex projects, several contractors working on the same project, matrixed or cross-functional teams, and multicultural organizations has radically changed the way we manage and, consequently, the skills required of project managers.

Not too many years ago, it was thought that as long as a person had strong technical skills, had demonstrated a certain amount of aggressiveness and enthusiasm, and had worked on several project teams for experience, he was made a project manager. Notice that I did not say that one of the characteristics had to be the ability to get along with others. Although that was a definite plus, it really was not considered a necessary quality to manage a project successfully. Notice also that I referred to the project manager as "he." Women in project management, at least to any large extent, did not exist until relatively recently—about 1985.

This chapter discusses the evolution of project management and the major skills of the most successful project managers.

Project Management as a Career Path

Until the early 1980s, the career paths leading to the top corporate positions were usually through finance or marketing. That path is changing rapidly, though, as more and more organizations adopt the project management concept as a way of managing their business. Project management is now recognized as a legitimate career path, and many organizations are choosing their top corporate officers from their project manager ranks. It really should not be surprising that a highly trained and experienced project manager would make a good top executive, since running a large, complex project is like running a small company; the project manager has to have broad experience in all aspects of an organization.

The organizations that are adopting the project management concept of managing their business are also going to great lengths to ensure that their project managers are highly trained. Companies such as AT&T, IBM, Bell South, and Citibank are sending project managers through rigorous training courses designed to prepare them for certification as a Project Management Professional (PMP).

The Project Management Institute (PMI) is the certifying body that bestows PMP certification. This organization was begun in 1969 by a group of concerned managers who sought to improve the quality of project management work. Over time, the organization has grown to approximately 20,000 members. The PMI membership has identified a body of knowledge, known as the Project Management Body of Knowledge (PMBOK), which represents the knowledge areas that a project manager needs to master before becoming a certified project management professional:[1]

- Project Scope Management (scope definition and planning)
- Project Quality Management (quality planning, quality assurance, and quality control)
- Project Human Resources Management (organizational planning, staff acquisition, and team development)

- Project Risk Management (risk identification, risk quantification, and risk control)
- Project Time Management (time in the sense of duration estimation, schedule control, and task interdependencies)
- Project Integration Management (project plan development, execution, and change control)
- Project Procurement Management (solicitation, source selection, contracts, and contract management)
- Project Cost Management (resource planning, cost estimating, cost budgeting, and cost control)
- Project Communications Management (planning, information distribution, project progress reporting, and other administrative requirements)

The point is that project management has become a serious career field, and one in which many large companies are willing to invest heavily in trained, professional project manager corps. Additional information about PMI and the project management certification process can be obtained by contacting PMI at:

> Project Management Institute
> 130 South State Road
> Upper Darby, PA 19082

Project Management Skills

Project managers can no longer depend on their positions or their initiative or their enthusiasm to accomplish the goal of a project successfully. Because most projects are managed from a matrix organization (see Chapter 10 for a discussion of various organizational forms), project managers have no functional control or authority over the project team members. Consequently, the project manager has to have strong interpersonal skills as well as technical and organizational skills.

Several years ago, Barry Posner, professor of organizational behavior, and managing partner of the Executive Development Center, Leavey School of Business and Administration, Santa Clara University, wrote a report on the problems of project management and the skills needed to cope with them.[2] Prior to Posner's study, there were essentially two views about the skills needed to run projects successfully. One school of thought held that the successful project manager needed to have a set of personal characteristics, such as aggressiveness, versatility, and decisiveness, to be able to accomplish the goals of a project successfully. On the other hand were those scholars who thought that it would be too hard to find people possessing all the requisite characteristics. Therefore, they argued that the emphasis should be focused on determining the critical problems of a typical project and then finding people with skills to fit the critical problems. Posner found, however, that these two schools of thought were not two different approaches but actually "two sides of the same coin."

Posner surveyed nearly 300 experienced project managers from across the country. The project managers were from various backgrounds and managed all types and sizes of projects. Posner asked two opened-ended questions in his survey:[3]

1. What factors or variables are most likely to cause you problems in managing a project?
2. What personal characteristics, traits, or skills make for above-average project managers? What specific behaviors, techniques, or strategies do above-average project managers use (or use better than their peers)?

Although the responders to the survey provided approximately 900 statements about the problems of project management, they all fell into one of eight categories. The list of eight project management problems, in the order of most often to the least often occurring problem, are shown in Exhibit 1-1. Not surprisingly, the most often mentioned problem is the lack of adequate resources and the next most often mentioned problem is the setting of unrealistic schedules.

Inadequate resources occur for many reasons. On the surface, the most obvious reason is that organizations are forced into having to do more with less in order to be competitive. Although that can be a contributing factor, in reality, it is more likely that inadequate resources occur because of poor planning

Exhibit 1-1. Problems most often encountered in project management.

---

1. Inadequate resources
2. Unrealistic schedules
3. Unclear goals and senior executive direction
4. Uncommited team members
5. Inadequate planning
6. Communication breakdowns
7. Goal and resource changes
8. Interdepartmental conflicts

---

or inefficient use of available resources. Whatever the reason, it is no less a problem to the project manager—he simply finds himself in the position of having to accomplish a project's goals when he doesn't have enough or the right people to do it.

Unrealistic deadlines occur all too often. Usually these are deadlines imposed by the organization because it is reactively responding to a need or because it is promising earlier delivery in hopes it will make the company more attractive competitively. Again, the project manager is stuck with the problem of accomplishing the project's goals sooner than is reasonable or, in many cases, possible.

The third of these problems, unclear goals and objectives, is to my mind the biggest problem encountered in project management. The most difficult task often is just determining what the customer wants. Many customers themselves don't know what they want, which usually results in several, expensive false starts.

The second question Posner asked relative to what skills make a difference in successfully managing a project yielded almost 1,400 statements from the responders. All of these statements have been categorized into six major categories and are shown in Exhibit 1-2. Note that five of the six categories listed deal with interpersonal skills. This fact points out exactly why initiative or position alone is no longer sufficient for successful project management. The majority of problems project managers

Exhibit 1-2. Skills needed to be a successful project manager.

1. Communication skills	4. Leadership skills
Listening	Sets example
Persuading	Energetic
2. Organizational skills	Vision (sees the big picture)
Planning	Delegates
Goal setting	Positive attitude
Analyzing	5. Coping skills
3. Team building skills	Flexibility
Empathy	Creativity
Motivation	Patience
Espirit de corps	Persistence
	6. Technical skills
	Experience
	Project knowledge

encounter are not technical but interpersonal problems. This means that project managers now have to be competent in a broad range of interpersonal skills if they hope to be successful.

The first essential skill is the ability to communicate. This skill is important in any endeavor but is absolutely crucial in project management. It has been estimated that project managers spend 90 percent of their time just communicating: with the project team, the customer, functional managers, and upper management.

One of the subcategories under communication skills in Exhibit 1-2 is "persuading." Although persuading can be loosely interpreted to mean negotiating, I prefer *negotiating* because it is a stronger term. The project manager spends a large portion of her time negotiating for resources or equipment or other support, and if she doesn't have strong negotiating skills, then her chances of being a successful project manager are greatly reduced.

One other important point of interest in Exhibit 1-2 is that "technical skills" is listed last. Although technical expertise is important, project managers do not have to be expert in the project's technical area. In fact, it is better that they be a generalist rather than an expert. The reason is that experts tend to be very narrow in their views. An expert leading a project is less likely to consider any other view than her own. The tendency is for this expert to believe her solution is the right one, and therefore the only choice. A generalist, on the other hand, is far more open to the views and suggestions of the team members. On balance, the results of projects led by generalists tend to yield much better deliverables than comparable projects led by experts.

Posner related the results of the two survey questions to show that they are not really mutually exclusive. Exhibit 1-3 shows how the skills and problems of project management are related to each other.

Posner's study succinctly states and categorizes the requisite project management skills needed to manage a project successfully. But it is worthwhile looking at the same subject from a slightly different perspective. That is, taking the personal skills from Posner and the areas of knowledge required by PMI for their PMP certification, we can see that today's project manager really does need to be a generalist and, more than that, a generalist with extraordinary interpersonal skills.

Exhibit 1-3. The relationship of project management skills and problems.

Skills	Problems
Communication	Communication breakdowns
Organizational	Inadequate planning, insufficient resources
Team building	Uncommited team members, weak interdepartmental interaction and support
Leadership	Unclear goals and senior executive direction, interpersonal conflicts
Coping	Handling changes
Technical	Meeting unrealistic schedules

Source: Reprinted from Jack R. Merredith and Samuel J. Mantel, Jr., *Project Management: A Managerial Approach* (New York: John Wiley & Sons, Inc., 1985, 1989, and 1995). Copyright © 1985, 1989, and 1995 John Wiley & Sons. Reprinted by permission of John Wiley & Sons, Inc.

Successful project managers need qualifications in four categories:

1. Personal characteristics
2. Behavioral skills
3. Business skills
4. Technical skills

The personal characteristics alone include a wide variety of competencies and innate characteristics, including these:

- Flexibility
- Leadership
- Communication
- Discipline and organization
- Decisiveness
- Negotiation

The behavioral skills in some cases overlap with the personal characteristics required. These skills include those dealing with how the person relates to others. In other words, having good communication skills means knowing how to be articulate and how to present information. But a lack of behavioral skills that make the person an active listener would render the communication skills less effective.

Business skills are a combination of technical and interpersonal skills. The technical side deals with organizational skills, marketing, business development, strategic planning, cash flow, and profit and loss. The interpersonal skills for this category are those that help the person teach or mentor subordinates so that they are better project and company members.

Summary

Project management has become a recognized career path in today's business environment. With more and more companies turning to project management as a better way of managing their business, they are also finding that their project managers need more training.

Not many years ago, a project manager was chosen because of his, and occasionally her, technical expertise and general enthusiasm or aggressiveness. Those days are gone forever. Today's project manager has to be a generalist with strong interpersonal skills.

This chapter has discussed these skills in an overview and as a precursor to the following chapters, which address these critical skills, both technical and interpersonal, in much more detail.

Notes

1. William R. Duncan, *A Guide to the Project Management Body of Knowledge* (Upper Darby, Penn., PMI, 1996).
2. Barry Z. Posner, "What It Takes to Be a Good Project Manager," *Project Management Journal* (March 1987).
3. Jack R. Merredith and Samuel J. Mantel, Jr., *Project Management: A Managerial Approach* (New York: John Wiley & Sons, Inc., 1985, 1989, and 1995). Copyright © 1985, 1989, and 1995 John Wiley & Sons, Inc. Reprinted by permission of John Wiley & Sons, Inc.

Chapter 2
Communication Skills

Good, the more communicated, more abundant grows.
—John Milton, 1608–1674, *Paradise Lost*

No other ability is more valuable to a person, project manager or otherwise, than the ability to communicate effectively with others. We communicate almost constantly and have done so all our lives. Why, then, should we be concerned about communicating if it is something we practice daily? The fact is that many of us don't communicate well, and even those of us who do can always improve our skills.

The word *communicate* comes from the Latin word *communis*, which means "common." The idea is to come together on a common ground of understanding. All means for transferring information, emotions, or thoughts fall within the purview of communication. Therefore, communication encompasses oral, written, and nonverbal means between two people. Nonverbal communication enters into both oral and written communication. Communication between machines or between people and machines also occurs, but our principal concern in this chapter is the communication that occurs between two or more persons.

The Project Manager as a Communicator

Although communication skills are very important to us all, it is easy to see that some situations require better-developed communication skills than other situations. For instance, effectively communicating in a social setting, albeit important, may not be as critical as effectively communicating during a negotiation session. In a social situation, the inability to communicate effectively would mean that one wouldn't be a popular conversation companion. In a serious negotiation, the inability to communicate could mean the loss of money or business. In other words, although effective communication is desirable in every human endeavor, it is crucial for success in some. Project management is one of those.

Project managers spend the majority of their time communicating. They hold meetings; report (orally as well as in writing) to the team, customer, or senior management; listen to problems; solve problems; and constantly negotiate with functional managers for resources. Project managers' success depends greatly on their ability to communicate.

In the project environment there are four types of communication:

1. Formal written (project charter, status reports)
2. Informal written (project notes, memos)
3. Formal oral (presentations)
4. Informal oral (conversations, team meetings)

In the formal and informal oral communication environments, the listening skills are employed as facilitative or as critical listening or both. The effectiveness with which these three skills of speaking, writing, and listening are used is important to the success of the project and the project manager.

The Project Manager's Problem: Potential Channels of Communication

The project manager has to deal with a large number of people: his team, functional managers across the organization, senior management, customers, customers' representatives, vendors, and still others. To put the size of the problem into perspective, consider this: The number of potential channels of communication available relative to the number of people involved can be expressed mathematically:

$$\text{Number of communication channels} = \frac{n(n-1)}{2}$$

For example, if there are four people in a group, the number of channels of communication will be:

$$\text{Number of communication channels} = \frac{4(4-1)}{2} = \frac{12}{2} = 6$$

And for a group of six people:

$$\text{Number of communication channels} = \frac{6(6-1)}{2} = \frac{30}{2} = 15$$

The potential lines of communication for a group of six people are graphically depicted in Exhibit 2-1.

Even for a relatively small project team of eight people, the number of communication channels will be twenty-eight. For each person added to the communication network, the number of possible communication channels increases geometrically. Relating this concept to the number of people with whom the project manager typically interacts on any given day, the possible number of communication channels is enormous. Clearly the project manager's communication role is the most far-reaching one, and one of the most important.

To understand the communication challenge requires that we first look at the general process of communication, that is, the process of sending and receiving a message.

A Communication Model: Sending and Receiving Messages

We often marvel at how the simplest messages can sometimes be received so differently from the way we thought they were transmitted. This phenomenon is the basis of the children's

Exhibit 2-1. Channels of communication for a six-member team.

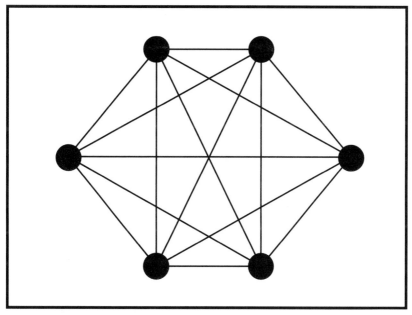

game of Telephone, in which one person starts the process by whispering a message into the ear of his neighbor, and the next person continues the process by whispering the message she thought she heard into the ear of her neighbor. When the last person repeats the message aloud, the ending message seldom resembles the beginning one. This transmutation of messages can be explained using a variation of the Shannon-Weaver model shown in Exhibit 2-2. The Shannon-Weaver model was first published by Claude Shannon in a Bell System technical journal and later included in a work coauthored with Warren Weaver.[1] (Their model did not include the feedback loop.)

From the exhibit, you can see that there are five parts to the communication process: (1) the messenger or message generator, (2) the message itself, (3) the channel or medium of transmittal, (3) the receiver, and (5) feedback. I include feedback in this process because successful communication occurs when the message is understood and accomplishes its purpose, and this

Exhibit 2-2. A communication model.

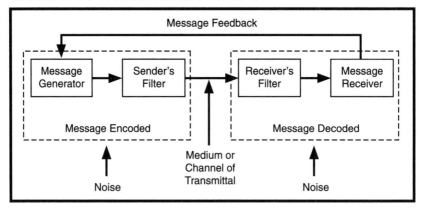

can be known only through feedback from the intended message receiver. In addition to these five communication components, there is outside noise in the form of distractions and other disturbances interposing themselves into the message channel.

Why Messages Go Astray

Each of us is a message generator or receiver depending on whether we are sending a message or receiving it. When a message generator attempts to communicate with another person, she first formulates a message in her mind. As this message is formulated, it is filtered with preconceptions about the intended receiver's ability to understand it. Sometimes the preconception is wrong, and the transmitted message is either too simple or too complex. Perhaps the language used is vague because of an assumed higher level of understanding or experience than exists. Regardless, the message is filtered through the generator's own experiences and background before it is put into the communication channel, and because of that, the message is already subject to misinterpretation.

The message generator also packages the message with facial expressions—a smile perhaps—or other body and voice tones that shade the message. Consider the difference in a message that is conciliatory on paper from the same message delivered verbally with a sneer and a sarcastic tone. This encoding of the message with distinctive body and voice characteristics has a significant bearing on how the message is received.

The receiver of the message has a set of filters similar to the sender. First, the receiver has to decode the body and voice packaging of the message and assess whether there are hidden meanings in the words. Then the receiver filters the message through his own experiences and background to determine whether the message is on a common ground of understanding with the sender.

On top of all the encoding, decoding, and filtering done by the sender and receiver of a message, there is added another complication: noise, that is, any distraction that is constantly at work during an exchange of messages. This distraction includes actual noise, such as loud talking, banging doors, and outside traffic, as well as irritating habits of the sender or receiver, such as mumbling, poor grammar, incomplete sentences, or biased or vulgar language. If the message is written, noise could be in the form of poor handwriting or poor spelling.

It is not hard to understand why messages go astray. The question is, What can be done to improve the process? To improve the process requires an understanding of the five processes of verbal communication.

The Five Processes of Verbal Communication

Verbal communications—those that deal with words, whether orally transmitted or written—encompass five processes:

1. Speaking
2. Writing
3. Reading
4. Listening
5. Thinking

The three of these that most clearly affect the project manager's ability to communicate and function in the project management role are speaking, writing, and listening skills. This chapter addresses each of these three processes in order and points out the problems encountered in each, along with some suggestions about how to improve them. Developing critical reading and thinking skills is also important, but is beyond the scope of this book. Some references are provided at the end of this chapter for those interested in pursuing these topics.

Developing Speaking Skills

If a professional project manager is asked to describe what a project manager does, the answer most often given is, "I get things done." J. Davidson Frame tells a story, which I have paraphrased, about an attendee in one of his seminars on project management:

> An individual told Dr. Frame that the seminar was interesting, but that he already knew all the techniques, and religiously employed them in all his projects. Even so, he just did not seem able to get things to happen. He feared that he would be relieved from his project soon if things did not improve.
>
> Dr. Frame spent enough time with the fellow to deduce that he was not very articulate, was clumsy in his human interaction, and was excessively didactic. Though the individual made an effort to ask for an opinion of what his problem was, he interrupted or contradicted every time Dr. Frame offered a suggestion.[2]

This scenario is repeated every day in the workplace because so few people understand the art of communication or don't try to improve their communication skills.

Since project managers must constantly communicate with a variety of audiences, and most of the communication is oral, the place to start is in the improvement of speaking and presentation skills.

Taking Stock

We usually are not our best sources for objective criticism, but it is beneficial to assess our own communication strengths and weaknesses. Some of the questions we need to ask, with as objective a view as possible, include the following:

- How clear is my speaking voice?
- Do I mumble or slur my words?
- Am I careful about the choice of my words? Do I use slang excessively or profanity? Do I ever use racial or sexually biased language?
- Do I use correct grammar?

Many people will be surprised at the number of bad habits they have because we don't often take stock of our shortcomings.

After self-assessment, it is beneficial to ask someone close—a spouse, parent, or sibling—to provide a similar assessment. With several data points you can develop and then implement a plan for improving your communication skills. Exhibit 2-3 illustrates this process.

Developing Presentation Skills

Project managers regularly communicate on a one-on-one basis, as well as in groups and to groups. Presentation skills are basic skill requirements that can be used in each of these settings, and they can be learned with a little guidance and practice.

There are several misconceptions that can stifle presenters. Thomas Leech lists six in his book on preparing and delivering winning presentations:[3]

Misconception I: You Have to Have a God-Given Talent to Be a Good Speaker

Although it is true that many people are blessed with an excellent speaking voice and personal demeanor, and have had the good fortune to have a good foundation in grammar, it cer-

Exhibit 2-3. Process for communication assessment, plan preparation, and implementation.

tainly does not mean that others not so blessed cannot develop these qualities. It is just as true that there are many people who do not have a particularly good speaking voice but are viewed as good speakers because of their ability to relate to and engage the audience.

Misconception 2: It Was a Lot Easier for Them (They Probably Don't Have Stage Fright)

Many famous actors and performers admit to having stage fright every time they perform. Barbra Streisand recently completed a tour after many years of not singing in public. She admitted that she had not performed because she suffers from severe stage fright, and the tour was something she felt she had to do in spite of the stage fright to demonstrate to herself that she could overcome it.

Misconception 3: Good Speakers Don't Have to Work at It

All good speakers work hard to prepare their for speaking, whether one-on-one or to a group, because they know that to be persuasive, they have to have a well-thought-out presentation, with an envisioned outcome, that they have rehearsed (at least in their minds).

Misconception 4: The Experienced People Don't Get Nervous Anymore

The misconception is much like the one on stage fright. Even experienced people get nervous. One experienced speaker quipped that the only difference in his early speaking days is that now the butterflies fly in formation.

Misconception 5: I Could Never Be a Good Speaker

Many people use this excuse to never try. Someone who takes the position that she could never be a good speaker doesn't run the risk of failing. The fact is that you may not be a really good speaker, but everyone can improve, and the effort to improve will be rewarded.

Misconception 6: I Tried Everything and It Doesn't Work, so It Is Futile

The last two misconceptions are by far the most devastating; the first one prevents the action, and the second one is the resignation to it. There is no doubt that breaking this pattern can be very hard. And there is no doubt that making a presentation before a group is harder than talking to one or two people. But project management is a profession that requires both: speaking one-on-one and to groups. The effort to break this pattern of not trying will provide the impetus to improve, and improving your ability to speak before a group has the added benefit of increasing your overall confidence and capability to deal one-on-one. These misconceptions about making presentations or speaking while in a group create an enormous amount of apprehension. Often this apprehension is strong enough to paralyze you into such a state that you can never gain enough courage to speak out in a group, much less make a formal presentation. Exhibit 2-4 provides some tips for overcoming apprehension about making presentations.

Developing Writing Skills

Close in importance to speaking skills for project managers are writing skills. A given in project management is that there will be a plethora of reports to do in addition to the constant requirements for oral communications. It should be obvious that developing these skills to the maximum extent will ensure the greatest project manager success.

There has been a steady decline in writing skills over the past forty years. With the advent of television and other electronic media, reading and writing have become less important. With the news available in vivid, graphical detail, there is little reason to bother reading a newspaper or news magazines. Similarly with the availability of the telephone, e-mail, and teleconferencing, good writing has become far less appealing or used as a means of communication. Although e-mail is technically writing, it is typically used as a fast query and response system, with little regard to grammar or sentence structure. In short, the electronic media have sabotaged good writing skills, and people are becoming less comfortable with the written word.

Ironically, even though almost everyone celebrates the information technology explosion, most businesspeople I meet are unhappy with their own writing skills, the writing skills of their employees, or both. No matter how much information technology takes over the workplace, the power of the written word cannot be replaced. Given the amount and variety of written reports required of project managers and the surge by many cor-

Exhibit 2-4. Tips for overcoming apprehension about speaking.

What to Do	How to Do It
Start small.	Find oportunities in small-group settings, such as church and civic or professional clubs.
Progress slowly; pick slightly larger groups as you gain experience.	Consider Toastmasters or other speaking clubs. Consider attending regional meetings of your church or club.
Pick a topic of importance to you.	It is much easier to talk about something you feel strongly about and know something about.
Prepare thoroughly.	Thoroughly research and practice every speech. Practice in front of a mirror; practice before a friend, colleague, or family member.
Speak as often as possible.	Practice *does* make perfect. Speaking as often as possible makes it easier each time to get before a group.
Scope out the environment.	Always go early to the place for the speech. Knowing the room and its arrangement makes the process more comfortable. Be sure audiovisual equipment is in place and working.
Talk to the friendly faces.	During the speech, find those faces that seem supportive and talk to *them*. Try to locate three or four around the room so that you seem to be encompassing the whole audience as you focus on the friendly ones.
Concentrate completely on the message.	Avoid the pitfall of worrying about what the audience is thinking about you, how you look, or your clothes. Focus only on the subject and getting your points across.

porations to adopt a project management concept of doing business, clearly the ability to write well is in great demand by employers. Finally, as Deborah Dumaine, founder of Better Communications, a Boston-based firm specializing in business, technical, audit, and sales writing workshops, points out, "Skill in writing correlates highly with the ability to think well—to analyze information, weigh alternatives, and make decisions."[4] This statement epitomizes what is required of good project managers.

Benefits of Writing

Aside from the general benefits of writing already noted, there are several others as well. One of the greatest is its aid in decision making. All of us talk to friends or family about decisions we are wrestling with, and we usually find that talking out the problem helps us to crystallize our thinking so that we can make a decision or plan of action. Writing can perform the same function. Many people find that putting their thoughts on paper helps clarify the project or problem they are mulling over.

Just as writing can benefit the writer, it can also benefit the reader. Some information is too complex or lengthy to try to explain orally, particularly over the telephone. Hence, a well-written document provides the reader with complex information in a logical and clear way that no other medium can.

Steps to Powerful Writing

Writing skills can be learned and developed just as speaking skills can. Although some people seem to have a gift—their words flow effortlessly—most of us have to work at writing. It is helpful to approach writing as a process. With a few steps to guide the process along, writing can become less tedious and much more productive.

One of the major challenges in writing is to be reader focused—that is, focusing on the reader's needs rather than presenting one's own agenda. Therefore, the following guidelines are developed not only to help make the writing task flow more easily but also to ensure that the writing is reader focused.

Write to the Top, Deborah Dumaine's book on writing for corporate success, is an excellent primer for learning writing skills in general.[5] She presents six steps in a systematic approach to writing, and I have adapted her approach to fit the role of a project manager.

Step 1: Analyze the Purpose of the Document and Its Audience

In the world of project management, many of the required reports follow predetermined formats. Often templates of the report are prepared ahead of time, and all that is required is to fill in the blanks. Although this approach ensures that reporting is standardized and saves preparation time, it can also create an attitude that the reports are routine. Project management reports may be routine in the sense of reoccurring on a regular basis, but they should never be considered routine information.

This step requires analyzing the purpose of the document and its audience as a result of answering the following questions:

- Why is this document important?
- Who are the readers of this document, and what is their stake in the project?
- What should this report convey to the readers?
- What is the breadth of the readers' understanding of this project now? Would an overview be helpful or required?
- How do I want the readers to react? What type of information or style of presentation of the information will guide their reaction?
- Of all the information that has to be presented, what is the one thing that I want readers to remember?

Step 2: Generate Ideas That Need to Go Into the Document

Too many people start writing without giving much thought to the document's content requirements. This approach

leads to writer's block or just frustration about the report preparation. It seems to be our nature to want to start on a project
immediately, whether the project is writing a report or managing the installation of a complex information technology system,
without first going through the planning stage. Nevertheless, all
the time spent in planning the writing is more than made up for
in the effectiveness, efficiency, and relative ease of completing a
comprehensive but concise report. One of the best ways to generate ideas for the document is to make an outline. It is simple,
straightforward, and applicable to all kinds of documents. In
the case of the typical, routinely required project management
reports, there will be a corporate policy about format and probably a template to follow. In such cases, using the outline method
for generating ideas is applicable, with the template headings
serving as major outline headings. Exhibit 2-5 is a typical report
template, and Exhibit 2-6 provides a sample of how to incorpo-
rate the template into an outline form.

Step 3: Organize the Ideas Under Appropriate Headings

Once ideas and information have been generated, organize
them under appropriate headings. This step should be done
without regard to the headings of the standardized report template because using the report headings may be restrictive. That
is, there may be information that the reader needs to be aware
of, but it wouldn't quite fit the template. Once the information
is organized under appropriate headings (or categories), then
you can transfer the data into the right template headings. The
objective in this step is to ensure that all pertinent data are included in the final report.

Step 4: Sequence the Ideas in the Document for Maximum Impact

This may be the key step in the process of writing the report
because it is the one that helps you concentrate the focus of the
report on the one or two most important points. Sequencing the

Exhibit 2-5. Typical report format.

STATUS REPORT

Project: Report Date:

Phase: Report Period:

Project Manager:

Summary of Progress:

Project Issues/Problems/Action Taken:

Planned Activities for Next Reporting Period:

Potential Problems/Issues During Next Period:

Recommendations:

Request of Action/Decisions:

Exhibit 2-6. Traditional outline for generating ideas for
project reports.

I.   Overview of Project Progress
   A. Summary of work planned
   B. Summary of work accomplished
   C. Attachments of budget reports
   D. Attachments of schedules
   E. Budget and schedule variances

II. Summary of Issues/Problems Encountered During This Period
   A. Statement of each issue/problem with action taken
   B. Summary of impact of each issue/problem on overall project budget
      or schedule

III. Planned Activities for Next Reporting Period
   A. Key activities with person/group responsible
   B Special milestones
   C. List and description of meetings planned
   D. Deliverables due

IV. Recommendations and Requests for Action
   A. Description of recommended approval or action needed (if any)
   B Approval chain
   C. Required action from each level

information means to examine all the information that has been
generated to determine the key points and then to place these
points in the most obvious part of the report.

Most people tend to write much as they think. That is, they
think in a linear fashion, from the first step in the process they
want to describe to the last. If they write in the same way, then
the most important piece of information will be in the last sentence. Most of the time, the last sentence should become the first
sentence in order to highlight the important point. Therefore,
once you have organized the information under the appropriate
headings of Step 3, examine it with the view of moving the most
important statements to the beginning of each heading.

Step 5: Write the First Draft

Using the information that now has been organized and properly sequenced, write the first draft, using the report template if one is required. Do not fall into the trap of trying to edit the document as you write this draft; this will only restrict the flow of ideas and hamper your efforts to include all pertinent information. Address each heading of the report as quickly as possible without regard to the amount of information being supplied. The objective here is to get as much distance from the document as possible—that is, to use the document to describe completely and thoroughly the problem, status, or whatever other message you need to transmit. More is better in this case, at least to the extent that free rein is given to your effort to be thorough in presenting all relevant project information.

Step 6: Edit the Document

Editing a report is considerably easier than generating it. That is why it is important to resist the editing process until last. Cutting out superfluous information, words, or phrases, and therefore making the document more concise, is easier to do from the complete document than if there is still a need to add more information. Having to add information as an afterthought can make the writing sound disjointed and disorganized. Follow the editing checklist in Exhibit 2-7 to ensure that your editing is thorough. In the final step of the editing process—editing for style, punctuation, and grammar—the best reference is still Strunk and White's *The Elements of Style.*[6]

Becoming an Active Listener

Listening is important. The average worker spends about 50 percent of his business hours listening, but research has shown that

Exhibit 2-7. Self-editing checklist.

Purpose of report	Stated clearly?
	Specific statement about needed action?
Information	Complete and accurate?
Sequence of information	Most important statements at top of report?
	Ideas and information flowing logicallly?
Attachments	Pictures or graphics attached to clarify information?
Paragraph/section structure	Sentences and paragraphs concise and brief?
	Topic sentence in each paragraph; one topic per paragraph?
Words	Free of acronyms or defined?
	Free of clichés and jargon?
	Active verbs used?
Proofread	Spelling checked?
	Grammar correct?
	Punctuation correct?

the average person listens with only twenty-five percent efficiency. That means that if 100 million workers each make a $10 listening mistake per year, the cost to business is $1 billion.

The authors of one research study concluded that listening is related to other communication abilities and to success at work. Better listeners, they found, held higher positions and were promoted more often than those with less developed listening skills.[7]

Barriers to Listening

The following story is told about Franklin Delano Roosevelt and his belief that most people are poor listeners:

Franklin Delano Roosevelt, 32nd president of the United States, found the polite small talk of social functions at the White House somewhat tedious. He maintained that those present on such occasions rarely paid much attention to what was said to them. To illustrate the point, he would sometimes amuse himself by greeting guests with the words, "I murdered my grandmother this morning." The response was invariably one of polite approval. On one occasion, however, the president happened upon an attentive listener. On hearing Roosevelt's outrageous remark, the guest replied diplomatically, "I'm sure she had it coming to her."[8]

President Roosevelt was right, though: Most people do not pay close attention to what is being said. There are several barriers to listening that make this so:

- Inability to hear because the speaker doesn't speak loudly enough or enunciate clearly
- Hearing impairment
- Paying more attention to the speaker's characteristics—clothes, words, voice, accent, and so on—than to the speaker's meaning
- Preconceived beliefs or opinions about the subject that preclude hearing the speaker's ideas
- Thinking of what to say at the next pause in the conversation
- Fatigue
- Noise
- Visual distractions, such as people coming into the room or into the field of vision
- Trying to think of two things at once
- Inability to focus on what the speaker is saying

One of the major problems of listening is that our thought processes move much faster that the spoken word. The average speaker speaks at a rate of about 130 words a minute, but our thought processes operate several times faster. Consequently, active listening requires concentrated attention on the speaker.

I was present at a victory party for Senator John Warner of Virginia while he was married to actress Elizabeth Taylor. Naturally, Elizabeth Taylor received a great deal of attention at the party, and I enjoyed watching her make her way through the crowd of people as they eagerly vied for a chance to talk with her. The one thing that most struck me was the way she gave her undivided attention to each person who spoke to her. By her concentrated focus on each speaker, she made it clear that whatever the person had to say was very important, and she was anxious to hear it. Being an effective listener requires this kind of concentration and focus.

Perspectives on Listening

There are two perspectives of listening that are found in the project manager's world: facilitative and critical listening.[9]

Keys to Facilitative Listening

Facilitative listening means listening well, being courteous and constructive, and reacting to the speaker in an appropriate way. There are several key strategies to becoming a facilitative listener (they are summarized in Exhibit 2-8):

Be prepared. Being a prepared listener is every bit as important as being a prepared speaker. However, being prepared to listen isn't always possible. That is, if the opportunity to listen is the result of an unexpected one-on-one encounter, there may be no way to anticipate the topic of conversation. But if the meeting was requested, know what the meeting is about and be prepared to respond appropriately. What I mean by being prepared applies more to opportunities involving prearranged meetings. A facilitative listener will have read the agenda and any other background material available before arriving at the meeting.

Listen to fit the purpose. The purpose of the meeting will signal what type of listening is needed. If an individual team member requests a meeting to discuss a personal issue, the facilitative listener will be prepared to be empathetic and listen with the

Exhibit 2-8. Strategies for becoming a facilitative listener.

Listening Strategies	Preparation Strategies
Be prepared.	Read all materials prior to any meetings.
Listen to fit the purpose.	Listen with the appropriate seriousness and concentration that the meeting deserves. Project progress meetings require greater attention than team social gatherings.
Allocate adequate time for the meeting.	Scope the meeting, and resist telephone or other interruptions.
Look past the speaker's external characteristics.	Don't let the speaker's clothes, voice tone, or message put you off. Focus on the speaker's purpose.
Listen to the speaker.	Force yourself to maintain eye contact. Don't be disturbed by other activities in the area.
Be a responsive listener.	Respond to the speaker by nodding or with other nonverbal signals to let her know that you are listening and understand.
Ask for clarification.	Ask questions to show the speaker you are interested and to make sure you understand completely what is being said.
Think before asking questions, be brief, and be concise.	Never dominate the discussion. Always try to make comments or ask questions that are relevant and insightful. Be brief.
Help the speaker toward mutual understanding.	Sometimes a speaker can lose track of what is causing a misunderstanding in the discussion. Be helpful by rephrasing the questions or adding comments that clarify the problem.
Listen with perspective.	Overlook speaker or presentation flaws. Focus on the important points of the message.

appropriate level of concern and support. If the meeting is a team meeting to discuss the status of a project task, then a high level of critical and interactive listening is required. If the meeting is for entertaining or recognizing a team member's work, then listening noncritically is called for. Facilitative listeners adapt to the appropriate level of listening to fit the purpose of the meeting.

Allocate adequate time for the meeting. There are few things more annoying than having members of a team move in and out of a meeting or for a person to interrupt a meeting to take telephone calls. In a busy environment, it is not possible to avoid all the interruptions; nevertheless, the facilitative listener and smart listener will allot enough time to complete the meeting with minimum interruptions. The benefit is to both the speaker and the listener.

Look past the speaker's external characteristics. We often tune out a speaker because we don't like his looks, his manner of speaking, his accent, or his message. The facilitative listener will look beyond all that to the speaker's purpose. The message may be needed information, pleasant or not, and by not giving the speaker a fair hearing, the message will be missed.

Listen to the speaker. Whatever else is going on around the conversation or in the listener's life, the facilitative listener will put it out of her mind and concentrate completely on the speaker. Concentrating in such a focused way isn't easy to do and requires effort. The next time you are talking with someone, take note of how hard it is to maintain eye contact and not look away to see who just came into the room or what made the noise outside. In a meeting, the eye contact should still be there, and listening to the speaker means not carrying on side conversations or reading the report you brought along.

Be a responsive listener. A good listener will always respond in some way to the speaker—a nod to show agreement or some other nonverbal body movement to indicate attentive listening. Mrs. Johnson, my high school math teacher, after explaining some involved mathematical manipulation, once grabbed my sleeve and shook it vigorously. When she was sure she had my attention, she asked if I understood the mathematical derivation she had just explained. When I said I did, she said, "Well, change your face!" What Mrs. Johnson was saying to me was that I wasn't being a responsive listener; I wasn't "changing my face" to indicate comprehension or even that I was listening.

Ask for clarification. One of the best methods of keeping yourself focused on the conversation, showing the speaker that you are interested in what is being said, and making certain that you understand what is said is to ask for clarification periodically. In a one-on-one situation, this is not so hard to do, but in a group, people are reluctant to ask questions for fear of appearing stupid. The fact is, if one person isn't clear on a point, then there usually are others who didn't understand it either. From the speaker's perspective, it is better to have a chance to clarify points early than to continue talking about something that is baffling to the audience.

Think before asking, be brief, and be concise. Whether in a group or in a one-on-one situation, the facilitative listener will wait for a convenient breaking point to ask questions or make comments and then will be as brief and to the point as possible.

Help the speaker toward mutual understanding. In group meetings, it is not unusual for a speaker to become confused or unable to see the solution to a snag in the conversation. A facilitative listener will help resolve this difficulty or problem by offering examples or rephrasing the issue. In a one-on-one situation, there will be times when one individual has some difficulty expressing himself, particularly if the problem is a personal one and talking about it is difficult. Making the speaker feel safe by establishing rapport and creating a climate of trust is the facilitative listener's role.

Listen with perspective. The facilitative listener will overlook any flaws or minor problems with a speaker or presentation to focus on the major points of what is being said. The good listener can separate the wheat from the chaff and focus only on the important points of the message.

Keys to Critical Listening

Critical listening is a different level of listening from facilitative listening, but they are not mutually exclusive. Facilitative listening can be thought of as listening in a way that helps the speaker present her message. *Critical listening* is listening to spot the flaws and to cut through the rhetoric to the heart of the issues. There are several key strategies to becoming a critical listener (they are summarized Exhibit 2-9):

Look beyond technique to substance. Everyone is familiar with the type of speaker who is so polished that no one can remember exactly what his message was but liked him anyway because he was so dynamic or spoke so beautifully. Politicians have the reputation of being able to speak in broad terms and clichés so that they are not pinned down to specifics. Critical listening cuts through this type of presentation and discards anything that was said that did not add value or substance.

Look for the importance of the ideas. Ask yourself, "What is the point of all this?" If there is no point, then discard the information. It is more often the case than not that the speaker is trying to make certain key points but sometimes has difficulty getting directly to the point. Question the speaker to determine where the presentation is going if that appears to be the case. Keep the speaker on track and focused on providing information that will clarify the points being made.

Insist on specifics, not generalities. Whether one-on-one or in a group, the critical listener will insist that the speaker focus on details and not hide behind general statements. The statement by a task leader, "We will make up the schedule slippage by the end of the month," sounds good, but asking how it is going to be done might reveal that there is no workable plan in place to do it. In the world of project management, there is no substitute

Exhibit 2-9. Strategies for becoming a critical listener.

Look beyond technique to substance.	Look beyond the glitz and showmanship and discard all that does not add value.
Look for the importance of the ideas.	Always ask yourself what the point of the message is.
Insist on specifics, not generalities.	Require the speaker to focus on details, not make general or vague statements.
Question the assumptions.	The end results are directly related to the beginning assumptions. Be sure to examine and question the assumptions to ensure the logic being followed is valid.
Demand evidence.	Ask the speaker to cite evidence for statements made as fact.

for one of General Colin Powell's laws: Pay attention to the small things.[10]

Question the assumptions. The end results are directly related to the beginning assumptions. In project management, assumptions are made all the time. The critical listener will always test the assumptions to ensure that the logic being followed is valid. Whenever a team member presents a solution to a project problem, be sure that the assumptions are clear and valid, given the best information available.

Demand evidence. The critical listener will always question the assumptions and ask that the speaker cite evidence for statements made as facts. Too many people present data or information based on unverified facts. The project manager's job is to make sure that each team member operates from the perspective that all facts are verified and any information provided by the team can be substantiated.

Summary

Communication is the basis of all human endeavor. How well we succeed is directly related to our ability to communicate, and this is particularly true in the world of project management.

Given the process of communication with its inherent problems of filtering by the messenger and the receiver, the noise that invariably intrudes into the process, and our own lack of understanding about the art of communication, it is not surprising that messages go astray. To mitigate these problems, we can strive to improve our verbal communication skills, particularly speaking, writing, and listening.

Notes

1. Claude Shannon and Warren Weaver, *The Mathematical Theory of Communication* (Urbana, Ill.: University of Illinois Press, 1949).
2. J. Davidson Frame, *Managing Projects in Organizations* (San Francisco: Jossey-Bass, 1995).

3. Thomas Leech, *How to Prepare, Stage, and Deliver Winning Presentations* (New York: AMACOM, 1982).
4. Deborah Dumaine, *Write to the Top: Writing for Corporate Success* (New York: Random House, 1989).
5. Ibid.
6. W. Strunk and E. B. White, *The Elements of Style*, 3d ed. (New York: Macmillan, 1979).
7. Beverly Davenport Sypher, Robert N. Bostrom, and Joy Hart Seibert, "Listening, Communication Abilities, and Success at Work," *Journal of Business Communication* (Fall 1989).
8. Clifton Fadiman, ed., *The Little, Brown Book of Anecdotes* (Boston: Little, Brown, 1985).
9. Leech, *How to Prepare*.
10. Colin Powell with Joseph E. Persico, *My American Journey* (New York: Random House, 1995).

Additional References of Interest

Buzan, Tony, with Barry Buzan. *The Mind Map Book*. New York: Penguin Books, 1993.
Silva, José. *The Silva Mind Control Method for Business Managers*. Englewood Cliffs, N.J.: Prentice-Hall, 1983.
Wonder, Jacquelyn, and Priscilla Donovan. *Whole-Brain Thinking*. New York: Quill, 1984.

Chapter 3
Negotiation Skills

Let every eye negotiate for itself and trust no agent.

—William Shakespeare

The skill employed the most by project managers but the one that is the least discussed is the negotiation skill. Considering that the work life of a project manager is filled with conflict, it is surprising that so few project management books present negotiation skills and strategies in any depth. Yet project managers have to deal with a variety of sources of conflict, and in a manner that does not alienate anyone. Developing this skill should be a high priority for project managers; if they aren't good negotiators, they should start looking for a new job.

This chapter addresses the primary causes of conflict in a project and the skills and personal qualities required to cope with the conflict. The chapter closes with a set of guidelines for preparing and executing a negotiation event.[1]

Sources of Conflict in a Project

H. J. Thamhain and D. L. Wilemon, organizational behavioralists and consultants in management issues, determined that conflict during a project life cycle stems from one of the following:[2]

- Project priorities
- Administrative procedures

- Technical trade-offs
- Staffing
- Support cost estimates
- Schedules
- Personalities

One or more of these areas will be the focus of the conflict, but the conflict itself typically is the result of a difference of opinion. Five groups of people have an interest in one or more of these areas of conflict:

- The customer
- Functional and senior managers
- Project team members
- Other stakeholders
- Vendors

Negotiating with vendors is usually the responsibility of a procurement or contracting staff member, not the project manager, so I will not address this area.[3]

All seven sources of conflict that Thamhaim and Wilemon identified are present throughout the project, but the intensity of each varies with the phase of the project. In Part Two, we examine each area of conflict, and I explain why they become more intense in one project phase than in another. In this chapter, we concentrate on identifying the parties at interest for each of the conflict sources and show how the project manager can deal with them.

The Customer

The project manager is the key contact person for the client or customer. The depth and complexity of negotiations with the customer vary according to whether the customer is external or internal to the project organization. If the customer is external to the organization, the project manager often is responsible for the proposal's leading to a contract award and sometimes participates in the contract negotiations. This kind of negotiation is far more complex and adversarial than that dealing with an internal customer. With an internal customer, the project manager is negotiating with friends and allies (this is presuming a congenial and collegial corporate environment). However, these two scenarios require the same skills, and the same negotiation guidelines, discussed later in this chapter, will apply.

The customer is interested in schedules, budgets, and product specifications. Hence, these will be the primary causes of any conflict between the project manager and the customer.

Functional and Senior Managers

The functional manager has control of the personnel resources that the project manager needs to staff the project. She must negotiate with the functional managers for these resources and must often battle to keep the resources assigned to the project when functional priorities change. The functional managers also have strong opinions about the technical approach of a project. The project manager similarly negotiates regularly with senior managers regarding project priority and their commitment.

Project Team Members

In working with the project team, the project manager acts more like a mediator than a negotiator. A team member might negotiate with the project manager to do one task that is more interesting or challenging than the one assigned. For the most part, however, the relationship between the project manager and the team member is more one of leader and follower. The real problem for the project manager in a team setting is to mediate between the team members and resolve any personality conflicts that occur.

Other Stakeholders

Other stakeholders include people who do not have a direct involvement in the project but do have an interest in it because it could have an impact on their function. For instance, someone from finance would not have a direct interest in the technical aspects of the project but does have an interest in how it affects cash flow or profits. A functional manager might not have any involvement in the project now but might have the responsibility for maintaining the end product. Dealing with these stakeholders requires the project manager to be part negotiator and part politician.

The wise project manager will determine all the stakeholders early in the project cycle and relate their goals to the project's goals. Most people avoid using the word *politics* when speaking of their job. The fact is, though, that polishing and exercising one's political skill is crucial to success, especially in dealing with stakeholders. The project manager's influence is fragile at best, and exercising her political skill is one way to build influence.

In his book on project management, J. Davidson Frame defines a three-step process that a good project politician follows:[4]

1. *Assess the environment.* In assessing the environment, the project manager must be sensitive to the corporate goals and strategies and who the relevant stakeholders are. The environment of the company is determined by the corporate culture and the company's current competitive status. If the culture is not a collegial and supportive one, then the project manager needs to exercise considerable political skill. Even if the culture is collegial and supportive, it is not unusual to discover at least one person who is against the project. When this situation occurs, it is crucial for the project manager to identify the person and try to assuage her concerns. An unhappy stakeholder can undermine a project before the unwary project manager knows what is happening.

2. *Identify the goals of the principal actors.* Once the stakeholders are identified, the project manager must ascertain their goals. What drives these people? Do they have a hidden agenda? If so, how can you deal with this hidden agenda? It is not easy to determine what drives some people. That is probably why many project managers, even professional project managers, do not bother with these steps. They jump straight into problem solving

and finding solutions. What they fail to understand until it is too late is that stakeholders can make or break a project. Making sure the project goals are consistent with those of the stakeholders is the surest way to obtain and keep them as allies.

3. *Assess your own capabilities.* Successful project managers know their own strengths and weaknesses and how best to capitalize on their strengths. Once the project manager identifies the stakeholders and their goals, he has to act to mitigate any negative feelings or reservations about supporting the project. Without an objective self-analysis and a critical evaluation of his own capabilities, he will find that dealing successfully with people's problems, particularly those external to the project, becomes impossible.

Once these three steps—assessing the environment, identifying the goals, and assessing your own capability—are accomplished, the project manager is able to define the problem and develop and refine proper solutions. It bears repeating that the nature of a project manager's influence is fragile under the best of conditions, and political savvy is one way to increase one's influence in the company.

The Skills and Personal Qualities of a Good Negotiator

Successful negotiators have three key skills—communication, listening, and judgment—and three personal qualities—honesty, flexibility, and credibility.

Honesty

Honesty is the single most important personal quality of a successful project manager. Almost every other mistake a person makes can be overcome and forgiven but not dishonesty. Once a person lies, no one fully trusts him again, and his influence and effectiveness are ruined. Nevertheless, many professional project managers will risk damaging their credibility and violate their integrity rather than admit that they are having a problem with a project. This is a serious failing.

Sometimes the project manager is caught in the difficult situation of being directed by a senior manager not to reveal a problem to the customer. The rationale is that the problem will be corrected without the customer's ever being the wiser. In this situation, you have to evaluate your ethical code and decide whether your conscience will allow the lie and if you are willing to risk your professional reputation.

Certainly some judgment is required about the seriousness of a problem. Every project has problems, but the problems we are discussing here are those that transcend the daily snags, irritations, and false starts. The customer will not be interested in these problems. However, if the problem is severe enough to cause a delay or requires a short-term infusion of additional resources, the customer needs to know about it. She will *not* be upset that the project manager encountered a problem. She *will* be upset to learn of the problem after it is so big that there is a significant impact on the project. The customer knows there are going to be problems in every project. Do not insult her intelligence by pretending no problems exist in your project; she will not believe it. Remember that the customer will accept problems as long as she can be a part of the solution.

Flexibility

Project managers usually work in a matrix organization: The project team members come from functional groups throughout the company. This means that the project manager does not have direct control over the company's personnel and must negotiate with the various functional managers for their use. Consequently, she must know what skill level is needed for the project, and there must be an alternative choice if the ideal candidate is not available to work on the project. Functional managers usually are willing to assign the requested person to a specific project, but that person may already be working on one or more projects. Hence, to have access to a particular person may require juggling schedules, taking the desired person for odd or random periods, and supplementing with other people. Sometimes a particular person may be available only for some supervisory duties or as a consultant to the project. All this requires the project manager to be knowledgeable about the goals and objectives, schedule, and required product quality and to be flexible in her approach to resource negotiations.

Credibility

Credibility means the project manager is known to be a person of integrity, knowledgeable, capable, and dependable. A reputation for credibility is earned; it cannot be established overnight, and it will not be believed until it is demonstrated. This quality is something that the project manger must work at with patience and persistence. The only way to be credible is to deliver as promised, be honest in all dealings, and be consistent in behavior.

If these words sound remarkably like those in the discussion about honesty, it should not be surprising. The two are not mutually exclusive. You cannot have one without the other.

Communication Skills

The project manager is the spokesperson for the project. I remember as an engineering student having to take a course that required researching a topic and formally presenting the results to the class; essentially this was a public speaking course, but oriented to engineers presenting technical information. One of my classmates complained often and loudly about having to take the course. "I'm going to be an engineer, not a public speaker," he protested. "I don't need a public speaking course." How wrong he was! People who can't communicate well are severely limited. In addition, people who are more proficient at communication are more successful.

Listening Skills

Being a good listener is key to being a good communicator. Many people seem to define communication as the art of speaking effectively but forget that good communication requires dialogue. They forget the other half of the communication equation: listening. Usually we are so busy thinking of what we are going to say next that we don't listen to what the other person is saying. Worse, periods of silence make us uneasy so we feel compelled to continue talking past anything meaningful. It is impossible to listen when you are talking.

Good Judgment

A colleague once told me that judgment is innate; either you have it or you don't. I disagree. Judgment is a skill that can be developed. Good judgment is based on knowledge of the subject, the ability to project what the consequences of the judgment will be, the ability for problem solving and generating alternative solutions, and the capacity for making decisions. Exercising patience and drawing on all the other skills of a project manager will enhance the project manager's judgment, and a system for making good decisions can be developed. There are four steps leading to good judgment decisions:

1. Study the problem or planned course of action.
2. List the potential risks and consequences of the decision.
3. Generate alternative solutions or modify the original solution.
4. Make the decision.

Good judgment means more than providing solutions, courses of action, or solving problems. It means knowing when and how to say no to unreasonable constraints placed by senior management or the customer. It means knowing when to tell the customer that certain new changes can't be accommodated within the current scope of the contract. It means knowing when to go to senior management for help rather than admitting a problem is beyond your current capability or control.

Negotiating Guidelines

Roger Fisher and William Ury's excellent book, *Getting to Yes*, is a superb negotiation primer that presents what the authors call "principled negotiation."[5] Principled negotiation assumes a win-win solution and thus must be the project manager's approach. When the project manager negotiates, she is negotiating with friends and allies, not adversaries, and the negotiations are for the long-term benefit of the company, not for any individual. There are four steps in principled negotiation:

1. Separate the people from the problem.
2. Focus on interests, not positions.
3. Create options.
4. Insist on standards.

I have expanded this concept to seven steps, which can serve as a checklist for negotiation preparations and execution. The principled negotiation steps are incorporated in the guidelines shown in Exhibit 3-1.

Step 1: Prepare

The project manager should be the most knowledgeable person about the project. Many projects are the result of a competitive bid in which a proposal was submitted in response to a formal, written solicitation called a request for proposal or invitation for bid. In those cases, there will be project specifications, a statement of work, a contract document, and a proposal that provides a complete project management plan. The project manager is responsible for having a thorough knowledge of each of these documents and should be prepared to explain any or all of them when she enters into negotiations with senior and functional managers, other stakeholders, and the customer.

A project that is assigned within the organization and does not have written specifications or a project plan requires special consideration by the project manager. She is responsible for

Exhibit 3-1. Guidelines for successful negotiations.

Guidelines	Strategies
Step 1: Prepare.	Know everything possible about the project.
	Profile the person with whom you are negotiating.
Step 2: Be sensitive to different perceptions.	Separate people from the problem.
	Understand that each person's view of the project may be different.
	Focus on interests not positions.
Step 3: Use creativity and imagination.	Create options.
	Be flexible.
Step 4: Help others to agree with your proposal.	Use standards, published procedures, and corporate goals.
Step 5: Value any deadlines you agree to.	Never violate the agreements made with functional managers and team members.
Step 6: Take notes and follow up with a record outlining the agreements.	Always provide a written record of the agreements each party made.
Step 7: Prepare for no agreement, but leave with an intact relationship.	Be prepared in case no agreement is possible.
	Leave every negotiation with the relationship intact.

writing a plan (the format and purpose of a project management plan is discussed in Part Two of this book) and collecting all possible data about the project's goals, scope, objectives, and budget.

Complete technical knowledge about the project is only half the preparation equation. The project manager should also identify the stakeholders and other functional managers she has to negotiate with and prepare a profile of each one of them before negotiations begin. Knowing all you can about the other people—their goals and how they view your project—before you meet with them is crucial for a successful negotiation.

Step 2: Be Sensitive to Different Perceptions

Every person will have a slightly different, and sometimes radically different, perspective of the project. Even after everyone agrees about the goals of the project, the approaches to reaching these goals will differ. The wise project manager will be sensitive to these different viewpoints and be open to them. Determining the interests of each person isn't always easy, but focusing on their interests and not on their stated positions leads to a faster agreement and usually enriches the solutions.

One of the most serious mistakes a negotiator can make is to attack his opponent, or in our case the functional or senior manager, customer, or other stakeholder, rather than the problem. Attacking the person only makes her defensive and resistant to any proposal. Concentrating on the problem and soliciting her assistance more often results in solving the problem for mutual gain. Remember that these people have their own agenda; although they may be interested in helping with your project, it probably is not their first priority. They have other responsibilities that take precedence, and they usually are already supporting several other company projects.

Step 3: Use Creativity and Imagination

Flexibility is the key to negotiating with functional managers for scarce resources. The project manager has a requirement for particular skills and will have certain people in mind for the tasks. However, the desired people may not be available at the optimum time, or at all, during the period of the project. In that case, you must be ready with other options to propose. For instance, perhaps the person you really want is available to provide guidance and support to a less experienced person.

Step 4: Help Others to Agree With Your Proposal

A great general once said that you should always build a bridge so that your enemies have a way to flee. You shouldn't view those with whom you negotiate as enemies, but building a bridge so that they have a way of retreating is smart. Helping those with whom you negotiate to agree with your position is building a bridge for them. The bridge allows them to modify their position and accept your recommendations.

Citing corporate goals and objectives and relating them to the project goals and objectives will make it much easier for a functional manager to accede to your requests for help. If the functional manager can visualize clearly how her involvement with the project furthers her goals and those of the company, she will work harder to support the project.

Step 5: Value Any Deadlines You Agree To

Winning the battle but losing the war is an old cliché but one that perfectly describes the consequences of not adhering to agreed deadlines. Remember that most of the time, functional managers have made adjustments in their operating schedules to accommodate your requests for resources. When you agree to release a person at a specific time, the functional manager is presuming that person will be available for other projects then. If you ignore the agreed-to deadline, then the functional manager may have no choice but to withdraw his support.

If you have agreed to certain deadlines but cannot meet them because of a change in the project, then continued use of the person or equipment must be renegotiated. This situation may create a new set of problems that have to be resolved. Addressing the issue with the responsible manager most likely will create an ally rather than an adversary.

Step 6: Take Notes and Follow Up With a Record Outlining Agreements

Most professional project managers I know fail to take notes during their negotiations and seldom follow up the discussions with a record of agreements. Usually this is because doing so is just one more thing they have to do in an already too busy schedule. Yet consider how often we think we have an agreement, only to discover later that one party interpreted the agreement differently from another. Also, it is worthwhile to have a record of agreements to ensure that you know when the functional managers are expecting to have their staff available to them for other projects. Finally, having the results of all your negotiations on record relieves you of the burden of having to remember everything. Your life is too busy to rely on memory, no matter how good it is.

Step 7: Prepare for No Agreement but Leave the Negotiation With an Intact Relationship

Perhaps the most damaging thing that can happen during a negotiation is the destruction of the relationship between the two participants. The reality of everyday business is that no company or functional manager has enough resources to accommodate every project manager's request. Consequently, there will be times when you walk away without an agreement to support the project. Unfortunately, too many project managers believe that their project is the most important business initiative in the company, and they take a rebuff as a personal affront. They often become angry and attack the person they view as uncooperative. Even if this project manager successfully reverses the original decision, imagine how successful he will be in future.

Remember Step 2, and separate the person from the problem. If you are unsuccessful in obtaining the support you need from a functional manager, remember that there will be another time when you need his help. Parting on good terms can only help when next you approach him for help.

Summary

The work life of a project manager is a life of conflict. Although conflict is not necessarily bad, it is an issue that has to be resolved by the project manager. Without excellent negotiation skills, the project manager has little chance for success.

Conflict in a project life cycle can be attributed to one or more of the following areas:

- Project priorities
- Administrative procedures
- Technical trade-offs

- Staffing
- Support cost estimates
- Schedules
- Personalities

To deal with the conflict areas of a project, the following seven steps have been developed:

Step 1: Prepare.
Step 2: Be sensitive to different perceptions.
Step 3: Use creativity and imagination.
Step 4: Help others to agree with your proposal.
Step 5: Value any deadlines you agree to.
Step 6: Take notes and follow up with a record outlining the agreements.
Step 7: Prepare for no agreement, but leave the negotiation with an intact relationship.

Following these guidelines will help you approach each conflict issue or situation with greater confidence, and they will ensure a greater chance for success.

Notes

1. The following two books are especially helpful to project managers: Roger Fisher and William Ury, *Getting to Yes,* 2d ed. (New York: Penguin Books, 1992), and David A. Lax and James K. Sebenius, *The Manager as Negotiator* (New York: Free Press, 1984).
2. H. J. Thamhain and D. L. Wilemon, "Conflict Management in Project Life Cycles," *Sloan Management Review* (Summer 1975).
3. The following books provide help on negotiating with vendors: James C. Freund, *Smart Negotiating: How to Make Good Deals in the Real World* (New York: Simon & Schuster, 1992); Howard Raiffa, *The Art and Science of Negotiation* (Cambridge, Mass.: Belknap Press of Harvard University Press, 1982); Max H. Bazerman and Margaret A. Neale, *Negotiating Rationally* (New York: Free Press, 1992).
4. J. Davidson Frame, *Managing Projects in Organizations,* rev. ed. (San Francisco: Jossey-Bass, 1995).
5. Fisher and Ury, *Getting to Yes.*

Additional References of Interest

Breslin, William J., and Jeffrey Z. Rubin, eds. *Negotiation Theory and Practice.* Cambridge, Mass.: Harvard Law School, 1991.

Fuller, George. *The Negotiator's Handbook.* Englewood Cliffs, N.J.: Prentice Hall, 1991.

Lewicki, Roy J., Joseph A. Litterer, David M. Saunders, and John W. Minton, *Negotiation: Readings, Exercises, and Cases,* 2d ed. (Burr Ridge, Ill.: Richard C. Irwin, 1993).

Ury, William. *Getting Past No: Negotiating Your Way From Confrontation to Cooperation.* New York: Bantam Books, 1993.

Young, H. Peyton, ed. *Negotiation Analysis.* Ann Arbor: University of Michigan Press, 1991.

Chapter 4

Leadership Skills

Leadership and learning are indispensable to each other.

—John F. Kennedy

The traditional view of management and leadership is that management is concerned with efficiently and effectively using a company's resources to accomplish the company's business, while leadership is more concerned with innovation, challenging the status quo, and broadening the company's outlook and capabilities. Managers try to get people to do work more efficiently; leaders try to get people to agree about the things that need to be done. As W. G. Bennis and B. Nannus (professors at the University of Southern California) so succinctly describe the difference between managers and leaders, "Managers are people who do things right and leaders are people who do the right thing."[1]

Project managers have three basic responsibilities in managing a project: to be on or under budget, to be on or ahead of schedule, and to meet certain performance criteria (the quality requirements as defined by the customer for the end product). Notice that this is a restatement of my definition of project management from the Introduction. Therefore, project managers certainly must have the management skills to accomplish the project's goals successfully. What many people don't recognize is that project managers also must be leaders. Leadership qualities have become even more crucial in an environment of organizational downsizing and the trend toward organizations that are flat or have fewer layers of middle and senior management. With downsizing, there is more work to do with fewer people, and there are morale problems resulting from feelings of job insecurity. With flatter organizations, the project manager is in a more visible position, and the project is more subject to senior management involvement.

There is an overlap of management and leadership. Clearly, not every manager is a leader, nor is every leader a manager. However, the more successful project managers I know exhibit a high degree of leadership capability. This is evidenced by the higher level of morale in one project team compared with another, the fewer problems encountered during the life of one project than occur in another, the ability of one team to finish the project on or under budget and schedule, and the high degree of customer satisfaction found in some projects and not others. These high-performance teams are sure signs of project manager leadership.

Types of Leadership

It is a simplification to say that types of leadership can be described as either autocratic and authoritarian or democratic and egalitarian. Clearly there are many variations of these two extremes, but I focus on these two because there are just two ways of changing a follower's behavior: A leader can alter the follower's information or knowledge about a task (the *autocratic* approach) or alter the follower's motivation toward the task (the *egalitarian* approach). An explanation of these types of leadership will suffice to make clear what the project manager should strive for in the role of leader.

A great many studies have contrasted the authoritarian and democratic concepts of leadership. (Several are listed at the end of this chapter.) Exhibit 4-1 provides a summary of the differences between these two concepts.

Bernard Bass, Distinguished Professor of Management at the State University of New York in Binghamton, writes that authoritarian leaders are more concerned about the tasks or prod-

Exhibit 4-1. Autocratic and democratic leadership skills.

Autocratic (or task related)	Democratic (or person related)
Authoritarian	Egalitarian
Product or task related	Person related
Persuasive	Permissive
Goal achievement oriented	Group maintenance oriented
Punitive	Nonpunitive
Directive	Joint decision making
Charismatic	Consensual
Closed discussion and decision making	Open discussion and decision making
Nonrewarding	Rewarding

ucts than about the employees: "The punitive task-directed leaders make all the decisions and discourage subordinates' contributions. Authoritarian leaders provide structure, information, decide what is to be done, make the rules, promise rewards, and threaten punishment for failure or disobedience."[2] These leaders depend on their position and knowledge of policy to regulate the behavior of employees.

A democratic or egalitarian leader will actively involve himself in the leadership role, but his emphasis will be on the employee and relationships. This type of leader is more interested in subordinates' contributions to the process or team, encourages consensus decision making, and seeks out subordinates' input before making a decision.

Effects of Authoritarian Leadership

When Authoritarian Leadership Is Better

Certain professions or certain situations require an authoritarian leader. The military is an obvious profession, where not only the authoritarian leadership style is required because of the nature and rapidity with which decisions have to be made, but it has been shown that military officers who established a high level of discipline were more likely to be rated much higher by their superiors.[3] Similarly, it was shown that U.S. Air Force air crews who received feedback by highly authoritarian methods exhibited greater improvement in performance.

When Authoritarian Leadership Is Worse

When authoritarian leadership includes punitive and disciplinary actions, productivity tends to deteriorate. Punishment increases tension in individuals and groups. Employees who are singled out for punishment exhibit resentment, and they tend to infect the rest of the group with their resentment. The leader suffers from a loss of respect and credibility, and the entire process begins to deteriorate. As the morale and performance diminish, the autocratic leader typically reacts by increasing pressure and threatening more discipline, thus hastening the demise of the project, process, or group. The wall plaque that announces BEATINGS WILL CONTINUE UNTIL MORALE IMPROVES is based on a degree of fact.

Effects of Democratic or Egalitarian Leadership

When Democratic Leadership Is Better

A study of supervisors in an aircraft factory found that they were characterized by adequate authority, communication downward, sympathy, lack of arbitrariness, and lack of hypercritical attitudes toward employees.[4]

These supervisors were rated by higher management as being more effective than supervisors who exhibited less democratic behavior. Furthermore, their subordinates exhibited higher morale and were more productive.

Generally, it is agreed that in a person-oriented environment, employees or team members are happier, and productivity is greater. Democratic leadership is effective in any team environment, provided the leader recognizes that his or her ultimate responsibility is to ensure that the team is functioning smoothly and productively. Fulfilling that responsibility can require the leader to make decisions outside the democratic process. Hence, a democratic leadership style is preferable in project management, but has to be balanced against the urgency of project requirements.

When Democratic Leadership Is Worse

Even good things can be carried to extreme. Two studies showed that a leadership style that consistently reinforces the correct performance of team members by approval and suggestions for improvement results in better performance and higher achievement than if they are permitted maximum participation, as in the democratic style.[5] Hence, democratic leadership without sensitivity to the individual's needs for fulfillment and achievement will have an adverse effect on the team. The challenge for the leader, then, is to balance his or her democratic leadership style against the team's and the project's needs.

Leadership Qualities Followers Expect of a Project Manager

An in-depth study identified a number of characteristics important in a leader.[6] Four characteristics were top: honesty, competence, forward looking, and inspiring.

Honesty

Honesty was the characteristic most often mentioned by those responding to the survey. In my years as a project manager working with Department of Defense customers, I also found that each time a customer had a complaint about a contractor's representative, it was invariably related to the perception that the representative was dishonest. Similarly, whenever a customer praises a contractor's representative, it is most often because of that person's credibility, the basis of which is honesty.

Project managers make a serious mistake when they attempt to hide problems from their superiors or the customer. A project manager who tells the customer that everything is fine in the project when it isn't risks losing the confidence of the customer or, worse, having the contract terminated. In my experience, the customer never minds that the project has problems. What the customer wants is to be a part of the solution.

Honesty is the cornerstone of credibility. You establish credibility by your actions. If you are honest in all your dealings, it will be obvious, and your credibility will be established.

Competence

Competence does not mean that the project manager is an expert in all the skill sets of the project; it means that the project manager is able to get the work done, can control the project, can successfully negotiate for the resources needed, and can work well with the customer and the other stakeholders in successfully accomplishing the goals of the project. In short, the project manager has enough depth of knowledge of the project to know whether the goals are being accomplished and knows how to keep the project moving toward a successful conclusion.

You can demonstrate your competence by learning everything possible about the project objectives, goals, scope, specifications, and contractual requirements. No one else should know more about the project than you. Otherwise, there would be no hope of successfully accomplishing the project goals, and a project vision could not be developed. Competence is a demonstration of knowledge in the form of judgment.

Forward Looking

In project management, forward looking means that the project manager can envision the end result. The project manager has to have a systems or holistic view of the project and be able to accomplish the project goals while meeting the company's strategic goals.

Most projects are highly complex. There can be hundreds of

separate tasks, and all of them have to be integrated. Without the capacity to see how these tasks fit together to form a whole, the project manager may not meet the budget, schedule, and performance criteria.

To become forward looking, you have to develop a vision for the project, and the vision has to be centered around the customer's requirements. You don't have the flexibility of deciding how the end product will look or work separate from the customer's specifications. However, because you are the one person on the project team who has a clear understanding of the goals, customer requirements, contractual requirements, company objectives, and how they all will be met, you can develop a vision from the amalgamation of this knowledge, the technical approach defined by these constraints, and the completed product as a result of putting all these elements together. It is this vision that the project manager develops and communicates to the team and all the stakeholders. The leader must exhibit that she or he has a vision and from it a defined direction for the project. A leader with an unclear direction or no direction won't be followed.

Inspiring

Without the ability to inspire a team to work together or to inspire ownership by each team member, the project will fail. After all, leadership is determined by the followers. It is they who will finally determine whether the project manager is a leader. The project manager must inspire the team to accept her as the leader, get buy-in on the project, and maintain a high morale level.

How do you inspire another? You have to be energetic and positive about the project. If a project is viewed as just a job, as it is in many organizations, the work tends to become mundane or routine. But every project is different. That is why project management can't be reduced to routine. Consequently, a project manager needs to have a vision for the project and to communicate this vision to each team member. Inspiring the team with a vision means that the project manager is a cheerleader, a morale booster, and a champion for the project.

Five Management Practices and Ten Behavioral Commitments of Outstanding Leaders

Leadership qualities can be developed. Some leaders exhibit certain personality or behavioral characteristics that set them apart or make it easier to become what we typify as a leader. Understanding these leadership characteristics makes it possible to develop into a better, if not outstanding, leader.

J. M. Kouzes and B. Z. Posner identified five management practices and ten behavioral commitments exhibited when leaders described their best leadership example.[7] I have adapted these practices and commitments, shown in Exhibit 4-2, to the project management environment.

Exhibit 4-2. Leadership practices and behavioral commitments of superior leaders.

Leadership Practices	Behavioral Commitments
Challenging the process	Search for opportunities.
	Experiment and take risks.
Inspiring a shared vision	Envision the future.
	Enlist others.
Enabling others to act	Foster collaboration.
	Strengthen others.
Modeling the way	Set the example.
	Plan small wins.
Encouraging the heart	Recognize individual contributions.
	Celebrate accomplishments.

Challenging the Process

Search for Opportunities

The project manager is more constrained in challenging the process than is a functional manager. The customer will have specific requirements that must be met, and the project manager will violate the verbal or written contract if she unilaterally changes the project goals or specifications. That doesn't mean there aren't opportunities for challenging the process. Two obvious areas to seek opportunities for change and improvement come to mind immediately. One is in the organization's process. Managing a project is difficult even when everything goes right, but invariably barriers to the project's progress occur because of outmoded or outdated policies and procedures. The project manager should constantly seek opportunities to force changes to the system to improve efficiency and team effectiveness. The second place for change opportunities is in the expected performance criteria of the project. Exceeding the customer's expectations is good business and good leadership.

Experiment and Take Risks

Experimentation and risk taking are anathema to project management. The constraints of budget, schedule, and performance have to be strenuously adhered to. Nevertheless, there are numerous occasions when hard decisions are needed about the technical approach, the type and skill level of resources, or whether to change direction if an approach isn't working. The easy way out is to avoid making these decisions or passing responsibility for them to a higher management level. It is a weak project manager who won't or can't make a controversial or unpopular decision. The project team, though, and the customer will soon view the person who can make these decisions as a leader and a credible manager.

Inspiring a Shared Vision

Envision the Future

The vision in project management is centered around the successful conclusion of the project, the customer's satisfaction with the product, and the fulfillment of corporate objectives. The project manager must clearly see the end result before the project is begun. Without a vision, a clear direction can't be established. Without a vision, collaboration from others isn't possible.

Enlist Others

Having a vision is important but without someone to share it with, it remains a vision and will not become a reality. Every superior leader will talk about how the vision was made a reality by teamwork. Early enlistment of the project team, the customer, and all the stakeholders solidifies the parties at interest into a united whole, and the project will progress with greater support and fewer problems.

Enlisting others should be a priority for the project manager. It requires that she have a thorough understanding of the project's goals, scope, specifications, and objectives, as well as an understanding of how the project fits into the business and strategic plans of the company. And it requires that she conscientiously approach each party at interest and communicate the vision to them in such a way that they cannot but buy in to the vision. This requires skill, knowledge, and patience: skill in communicating the vision, knowledge about the project, and patience to continue to sell the vision when some of the parties at interest don't share enthusiasm for the project.

Enabling Others to Act

Foster Collaboration

The surest path to failure is to ignore building a collaborative team spirit. Since followers define leadership, it is incumbent on the project manager to forge relationships and foster and encourage collaboration among all the team members.

Amazingly, some people still believe in management by intimidation and think that a team can be bullied into top performance. Even if a project gets done utilizing the intimidation management method, the toll on the team is horrendous, and the long-term costs to the organization are stiff in terms of morale and employee retainability. On the other hand, management that is too laid back is equally devastating. Collaboration—fostering a cooperative spirit toward achieving common goals—is in the middle of these two extremes. It is the first step in enabling team members to function at the peak of their capability.

Strengthen Others

Strengthening others is daunting for some project managers because it appears to be giving up control or power. When a team member is enabled by giving him responsibility and authority to perform designated functions, the individual and the team are strengthened. Project managers also discover that rather than losing control by passing down responsibility and authority, they actually gain more control. Enabling team members fosters collaboration, which translates into power for the project manager. Real power in a leader is stronger if the power is bestowed by the followers than if it results from position. Hence, everyone gains. Strengthening the team member strengthens the team and the project manager—an unstoppable combination for achieving project goals.

Modeling the Way

Set the Example

Leading by example should be the self-evident mode of management. Nevertheless, all too often we find people in leadership positions who think the way to manage is to bully or cajole or otherwise intimidate. Usually this type of behavior is characteristic of an insecure person. Knowing that helps us to deal with the person, but how should we act as leaders?

Leading by example isn't easy. It requires being "on" more often perhaps than we would like. Leading by example means being consistent, being willing to do what you ask others to do, and fostering and practicing high ethical standards. In short, it means being and acting the way you want your team to be and act.

Plan Small Wins

People and teams react positively when they win. Planning a project so that the team works toward achievable goals is a natural for project management. Projects are generally too complex and run too long to plan in large phases. To be sure, there has to be an overall plan, a master plan, that clearly establishes milestones, goals, and schedules. However, a good project manager will use what is sometimes referred to as a sliding planning window (see Exhibit 4-3). This concept breaks the project into small, manageable segments—project phases, discrete time lengths, milestone-to-milestone increments, or a combination of these—that are thoroughly planned. How the segments are defined is not so important. What is important is that the segment be long enough to offer a challenge but short enough to visualize and achieve an end to it. These discrete wins will serve to build team morale and build a collaborative spirit among all who are involved with the project.

Encouraging the Heart

Recognize Individual Contributions

Every person wants and needs to be acknowledged. Small acknowledgments of good work done result in large performance boosts. Superior leaders give credit where credit is due and reap enormous benefits in the form of loyalty and even devotion.

Acknowledging performance demonstrates a caring spirit. Individuals and teams react positively when they have proof

Exhibit 4-3. Sliding planning window.

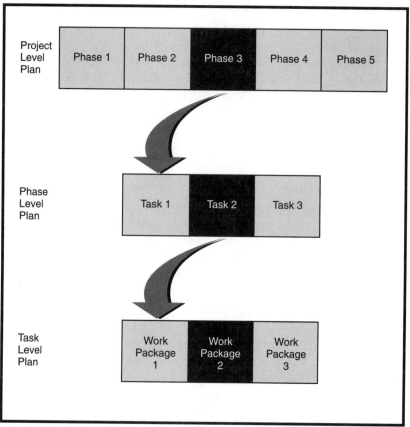

that the leader cares how they perform. The reverse is also true: If a leader doesn't acknowledge performance, the individual feels the leader doesn't care, and her performance will deteriorate.

Acknowledging performance is important, but just as important is how it is acknowledged. Performance should be rewarded, with the level of reward commensurate with the accomplishment. Sometimes it is sufficient just to acknowledge by name and deed the accomplishment in a staff meeting. Some accomplishments are big enough and important enough to reward with a dinner for two, a paid weekend at a nearby resort, or a cash bonus. Many companies give their project managers the authority to make such awards. Be sure you check the policies on this at your company and if none exist, suggest they be implemented.

Celebrate Accomplishments

Finally, every leader needs to make it possible for the whole team to celebrate accomplishments. The celebrations often will be spontaneous when one person or the team accomplishes something extraordinary or unexpectedly. Perhaps someone makes a breakthrough in the technical approach that had bogged down.

Project teams should also have scheduled celebration activities. Special holidays are obvious choices, but regularly scheduled events will show the team that the leader cares. They also bond the team. The feeling that everyone is working together develops, and pride of ownership of the project and the pride of belonging to the team will build morale and foster collaboration.

Summary

There are two leadership extremes: authoritarian or autocratic, which is more concerned with the task, and democratic or egalitarian, which is oriented toward relationships. Generally the autocratic style works only in special situations. For instance, the military is built on the autocratic style of leadership and this has to be so because of the nature and rapidity with which orders have to be given and unthinking reaction results. In other work environments, the autocratic style tends to create tension, dislike for the supervisor, and a significant reduction in performance. The democratic style of leadership, on the other hand, generally leads to high morale and high performance.

Studies by Kouzes and Posner reveal what followers look for in leaders.[8] Although there are a number (approximately twenty) of characteristics that followers look for, the four most important ones are that the leader be honest, competent, forward looking, and inspiring.

Kouzes and Posner's studies also reveal five practices and ten behavioral commitments that a leader can practice to ensure that individual expectations from the leader's behavior are met and that the team's performance is maximized. These five practices and ten behavioral commitments are:

Challenge the Process

1. Search for opportunities.
2. Experiment and take risks.

Inspire a Shared Vision

3. Envision the future.
4. Enlist others.

Enable Others to Act

5. Foster collaboration.
6. Strengthen others.

Model the Way

7. Set the example.
8. Plan small wins.

Encourage the Heart

9. Recognize individual contributions.
10. Celebrate accomplishments.

Notes

1. W. G. Bennis and B. Nannus, *Leaders: The Strategies for Taking Charge* (New York: Harper & Row, 1985).
2. Bernard M. Bass, *Bass and Stogdill's Handbook of Leadership*, 3d ed. (New York, Free Press, 1990).
3. Ibid.
4. A. L. Comrey, W. S. High, and R. C. Wilson, "Factors Influencing Organizational Effectiveness. VI. A Survey of Aircraft Supervisors," *Personnel Psychology* (1955).

5. R. C. Ziller, "Four Techniques of Group Decision Making Under Uncertainty," *Journal of Applied Psychology* (1957); P. Spector and B. J. Suttell, *Research on the Specific Leader Behavior Patterns Most Effective in Influencing Group Performance* (Washington, D.C.: American Institute for Research, 1957).
6. James M. Kouzes and Barry Z. Posner, *The Leadership Challenge* (San Francisco. Jossey-Bass, 1989).
7. Ibid.
8. Ibid.

Additional References of Interest

Bass, B. M. "Some Effects on a Group of Whether and When the Head Reveals His Opinion." *Organizational Behavior and Human Performance* 2 (1971): 375–382.

Hemphill, J. K., and C. W. Westie. *An Exploratory Study of Relations Between Perceptions of Leader Behavior, Group Characteristics, and Expectations Concerning the Behavior of Ideal Leaders.* Columbus: Ohio State University, Personnel Research Board, 1937.

Jaques, E., and S. Clement, *Executive Leadership.* Arlington, Va.: Cason Hall & Co. Publishers, 1991.

Katz, D., N. Maccoby, and N. C. Morse, *Productivity, Supervision, and Morale in an Office Situation.* Ann Arbor: University of Michigan, Institute for Social Research, 1950.

Lewin, K., and R. Lippitt. "An Experimental Approach to the Study of Autocracy and Democracy: A Preliminary Note." *Sociometry* 1 (1938): 292–300.

McGregor, D. *The Human Side of Enterprise.* New York: McGraw-Hill, 1960.

———. *Leadership and Motivation.* Cambridge, Mass.: MIT Press, 1966.

Misumi, J. *The Behavioral Science of Leadership. An Interdisciplinary Japanese Research Program.* Ann Arbor: University of Michigan Press, 1985.

Wofford, J. C. "Factor Analysis of Managerial Behavior Variables." *Journal of Applied Psychology* 54 (1970): 169–173.

Yukl, G. A. "Toward a Behavioral Theory of Leadership." *Organizational Behavior and Human Performance* 6 (1971): 414–440.

———. *Leadership in Organizations.* 3d ed. Englewood Cliffs, N.J.: Prentice Hall, 1994.

Section II: The Technical Tools

Chapter 5

The Work Breakdown Structure

The project WBS is the heart . . . the framework on which the project is built.
—S. E. Stephanou and M. M. Obradovitch, *Project Management, System Development, and Productivity*

The work breakdown structure (WBS) is perhaps the most useful tool of project management. It takes a variety of forms and serves a variety of purposes. When done correctly, the WBS is the basis for project planning, scheduling, budgeting, and controlling.

In spite of its value, though, many writers give little attention to the WBS and scarcely make mention of its use.[1] A WBS is not the only way to plan a project, and as long as some disciplined and detailed method for planning is used, then the project can be successfully managed. However, the WBS is such a fundamental requirement of many customers and can be used to such powerful advantage that a project manager would be wise to make developing a WBS his first priority.

One of the reasons that the WBS is not more widely used is that the concept is not well understood. Even writers who do espouse the virtues of WBS do not clearly explain the elements of it and how to develop them. The fact is that the literature is vague, often inconsistent, and usually incomplete about WBS development. It is not surprising that the WBS is too difficult and too frustrating to use, but this does not have to be the case.

Developing a WBS is not particularly easy, especially for complex projects. This chapter provides a simple approach that will facilitate the process.

What Is a WBS?

The WBS provides the basis of a plan for the successful accomplishment of project objectives. It is a structured way of decomposing a project into its various components: hardware, software, services, documentation, labor, testing, delivery, and installation. In short, the WBS is a formalized way of reducing the project into successively lower levels of greater detail.

The project decomposition should continue only to the level that is needed to identify the task or subtask as a *work package*, a natural subdivision of a cost account. It is a job assignment that is identifiable with a person, a job, or a budget number and is where the actual project work is accomplished. The work package can occur anywhere below the first level but usually occurs at the fifth level. *Levels* refer to the successively lower tiers of detail, beginning with the project name as the first level. The WBS almost never needs to be developed below the fifth level.

Think of WBS development as similar to a flowcharting process, except that we start with the project and decompose it into progressively smaller elements until the desired level of detail is achieved. Flowcharting usually starts with the most detailed or basic element and charts the steps toward the end or final product. The thought process for both, however, is linear and requires that each successive step be sequential, logical, and at the appropriate level of detail. If the WBS is viewed in this manner, it is easier to identify the project components.

The two most common forms for WBS presentation are the indented format and the graphical or tree form. The *indented* format, shown in Exhibit 5-1, derives its name from the practice of indenting each project level to delineate between and identify each of the levels. It is the most popular WBS format—the one used by all the project management software packages and is required when specified in Requests for Proposals or Requests

Exhibit 5-1. Indented WBS format.

```
1.0 Project or Contract Name
    1.1 Major Project Subsystem 1
        1.1.1 Task 1
            1.1.1.1 Subtask 1
                1.1.1.1.1 Work Package 1

        1.1.2 Task 2
            1.1.2.1 Subtask 1
            1.1.2.2 Subtask 2
                1.1.2.2.1 Work Package 1
                1.1.2.2.2 Work Package 2

    1.2 Major Poject Subsystem 2
        1.2.1 Task 1
            1.2.1.1 Subtask 1
                1.2.1.1.1 Work Package 1
                    1.2.1.1.1.1 Components

    1.3 Major Project Subsystem 3
```

for Quotes. The *graphical* format, shown in Exhibit 5-2, resembles a traditional organizational chart. It is an effective format for those who work better from visual presentations of data. However, it does take a lot of space to develop, particularly for large, complex projects.

Analyzing the Breakdown Structure

The WBS Levels

The project or the contract name is always level 1 of the WBS. (Exhibit 5-3 shows the format with explanations.) In the literature, the first level is often called the Program, with level 2 called the Project. However, this nomenclature is confusing because the term *Program* generally is interpreted to mean a collection of

Exhibit 5-2. Graphical WBS format.

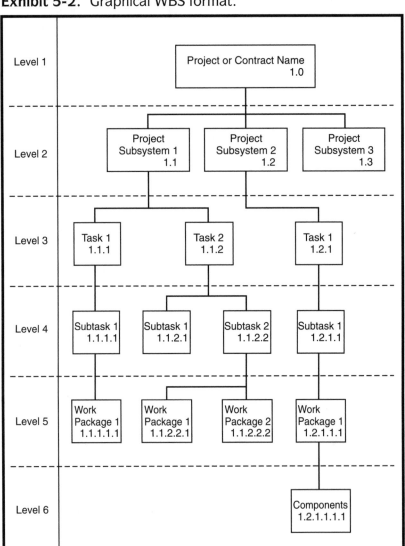

several projects with similar characteristics. Except in very rare cases, though, a project manager will by concerned with only one discrete project at a time, and each project will have its own WBS. Therefore, to eliminate the semantic confusion created by using *program*, always designate the name of the project as the

Exhibit 5-3. Indented WBS format with explanations.

Numbering Element	Description	Levels	Type of Format
1.0	Project or Contract Name	1	Managerial
1.1	Major Project Subsystem	2	Managerial
1.1.1	Task	3	Managerial
1.1.1.1	Subtask	4	Technical
1.1.1.1.1	Work package	5	Technical
1.1.1.1.1.1	Components	6	Technical

level 1 entry in the WBS. Then there will never be any doubt about what levels 1 and 2 should be.

Level 2 is composed of the major subsystems of the project— complete entities or sections of the project. The level 2 entries for an automobile design project, for example, would be the engine, the chassis, the interior, and the body, all of them complete subsystems of the automobile. Or suppose the project is to design, develop, and build a human centrifuge training system. The project name (level 1) of the WBS would be Human Centrifuge Trainer Contract. The major subsystems are the training device itself, technical support data (e.g., engineering data, administrative reports, logistics reports), the project management function, logistics support, and field services such as maintenance. Each of these subsystems will be a level 2 entry of the WBS.

Each level 2 entry can also consist of one or more major task activities. For instance, under the training device, there are systems engineering, hardware, electrical and mechanical design, and software design. These are designated as *level 3* activities, each of which can be decomposed into several more discrete activities and so on until the desired level of detail is achieved.

For example, the level 3 activity, mechanical design, might be divided into several subtasks such as the support axis design, cockpit shell design, and cockpit interior design. These level 3 activity subtasks are entered into the WBS at level 4. Continuing the process, the level 4 activity, support axis design, now can be expanded to a level where actual work can be assigned. That is, discrete work packages for preparing engineering drawings, analyzing structural strength, manufacturing structural members, and so on can be assigned to particular individuals or groups. The work package is level 5 and usually the lowest level ever required. Level 6 deals with components such as screws, computer chips, or other off-the-shelf items that are needed, but not usually tracked by the project manager.

Exhibit 5-4 shows a small portion of the human centrifuge example. The actual WBS from which the example is taken is five pages in length. Note in Exhibit 5-4 that some of the activities are expanded to level 5 while others are expanded to only level 4. There are two points to remember from this: (1) All activities in a WBS do not have be expanded to the same level, and (2) it is not required to go to level 5 to define a work package. Often, an activity only has to be expanded to level 4 or even level 3. The idea is to use the WBS as a tool to define the project work, and the activities should be expanded only to the level required to clearly do that.

The WBS Numbering System

The literature often does not adequately explain the importance of numbering the project activities. The numbering system can be numeric, alphabetic, or a combination of the two. The important point is that the first number is the number assigned to the project and is used by most companies as a means of tracking project costs and progress with the company's accounting and scheduling system. The first number does not have to be 1.0. Let's say the human centrifuge project is the fifty-first project of 1998. Someone in the company who tracks projects might assign the number 5198 to it so that it has both a unique designator (51) and shows how many projects were stated to date in 1998. Hence, the level 1 entry becomes *5198.0 Human Centrifuge Trainer Contract*. A level 2 entry would then be 5198.1, and so on. Every other digit place can also have unique designators composed of numeric, alphabetic, or a combination in the scheme. For instance, the designator 5198.A14.20 is interpreted as the twentieth subtask of the fourteenth task under the major project component in project 5198.

Exhibit 5-4. Section of a work breakdown structure for a human centrifuge contract.

1.0 Human Centrifuge Trainer Contract
  1.1 Training Device
    1.1.1 Systems Engineering
      1.1.1.1 Write Systems Engineering Management Plan
      1.1.1.2 Develop Systems Detail Design Specification
        1.1.1.2.1 Perform System Requirements Anaysis
      1.1.1.3 Develop Hardware System Design Specifications
      1.1.1.4 Develop Software System Design Specifications
      1.1.1.5 Do Reliability/Maintainability Engineering
        1.1.1.5.1 Write Safety Engineering Plan
        1.1.1.5.2 Write Human Factors Engineering Plan
        1.1.1.5.3 Write Reliability Engineering Plan
        1.1.1.5.4 Write Maintainability Engineering Plan
        1.1.1.5.6 Perform Preliminary Stress Analysis
        1.1.1.5.7 Write EMC (Electromagnetic Compatability) /EMI (Electromagnetic Interference) Engineering Plan
      1.1.1.6 Develop Support Facility Design Specifications
        1.1.1.6.1 Determine Systems Control Methods
        1.1.1.6.2 Develop Hardware and Software Interfaces Plan
        1.1.1.6.3 Prepare Site Plans and Facility Drawings
        1.1.1.6.4 Perform Electric Power and Duty Cycle Analyses
    1.1.2 Hardware, Electrical, and Mechanical Design
      1.1.2.1 Design Student Station
        1.1.2.1.1 Design Support Axis
        1.1.2.1.2 Design Cockpit Shell
        1.1.2.1.3 Design Cockpit Interior
    1.1.3 Detailed Software Design
      1.1.3.1 Develop System Program
      1.1.3.2 Develop Simulation Program
        1.1.3.2.1 Write Executive Program
        1.1.3.2.2 Write G Loading Control Algorithms
      1.1.3.3 Develop Instruction on Control Programs
        1.1.3.3.1 Write Lessons for General Systems Controls
        1.1.3.3.2 Write Lessons for Trainer Mode Controls
        1.1.3.3.3 Write Lessons for Emergency Controls
      1.1.3.4 Write Lesson Database Programs
        1.1.3.4.1 Develop and Write Beginner Scenario
        1.1.3.4.2 Develop and Write Advanced Scenario
        1.1.3.4.3 Develop and Write Custom Scenario
      1.1.3.5 Develop Utility Program
        1.1.3.5.1 Write Computer Diagnostics Program
        1.1.3.5.2 Write Operations Readiness Tests
        1.1.3.5.3 Write Real-Time Interface Diagnostics Program
  1.2 Project Management
    1.2.1 Project Manager
      1.2.1.1 Project Engineer
      1.2.1.2 Cost Analyst
      1.2.1.3 Clerical Support

You can quickly grasp why careful attention to the numbering scheme is important for tracking and accounting procedures and why a consistent numbering hierarchy should be practiced. Many writers correctly identify the project name as the first WBS level but then start the numbering system with the second level. In these cases, they also do not indent the second level so that our example would be shown as:

Human Centrifuge Trainer Contract
1.0   Training Device
    1.1   Systems Engineering
        1.1.1   Systems Engineering Management Plan

    1.2   Hardware, Electrical, and Mechanical Design

The problem with this procedure is that the "Training Device" and "Hardware, Electrical, and Mechanical Design" entries appear in the first-level positions, which is inconsistent with conventional practice. This numbering scheme therefore confuses the budget and tracking system. To be consistent with the convention and to facilitate tracking, the project name should *always* be designated as the first-level entry. In so doing, there will only be one first-level entry for each project. In addition, anyone can immediately identify an activity's level, even when taken out of context, because all succeeding levels after level 1 are identified by the number of digit places. For instance, we know the entry "1.1.2.1. Student Station" from Exhibit 5-4 is a fourth-level activity because there are four digit positions in its number.

Types of WBS Activity Entries

The first three levels in WBS are typically managerial levels (see Exhibit 5-3). That is, each level represents a management level and not a level at which the work is actually accomplished. The third level, "Task," usually represents a task leader position— the person responsible for supervising the task. Remembering those designations will facilitate decomposing the project into lower, and more detailed, levels.

The last three levels are where the work is actually accomplished. The subtask level might be composed of several work packages, so level 4 might be the system integration level. For instance, one of the level 4 entries might be to design databases for various scenarios in our example. One of the databases might be for a beginning pilot, another might be more advanced, including air combat maneuvers, a third might be customized for the particular user. Hence, each of these separate databases is developed by a person or team, and then they are integrated into a central computer system.

Level 5, the work package level, is usually the lowest level of detail ever needed in a project WBS because the next level, level 6, describes such things as the production of computer chips and screws, which would not need to be tracked.

WBS Element Description

One final word about how to describe these entries might help in the WBS development. If in the first three levels are described by nouns and the last three with an action word, it will be clear what type of activity goes in each level. In Exhibit 5-4, note that beginning with level 4, the technical levels, each entry begins with an action word denoting what sort of work is actually accomplished.

WBS Uses

The WBS can be used for a variety of work. Some important uses are as a basis for assigning task responsibility, project costing, network analysis, scheduling, and project control.

Assigning Task Responsibility

Assigning task responsibility is one of the most important uses of the WBS. The completed WBS will expose all the component parts of the project down to a workable level of detail. Once this is done, it will be self-evident who should do each piece of work and who should supervise each effort. The project manager, in coordination with the appropriate functional managers, will develop a task responsibility matrix, assigning a name to each of the WBS elements. This task responsibility matrix then shows at a glance who is responsible for every piece of work on the project.

Project Costing

The second most important use of the WBS is project costing. It is virtually impossible to estimate the cost of a project by viewing the project as a whole. Clearly the project has to be reduced to smaller elements until the cost of each element can be determined. As the cost of each smaller element is determined, the costs are "rolled up," to obtain one number for the whole project. The WBS is the perfect tool for this purpose since it decomposes the project into sufficient detail that the cost of each element can be determined.

I always include the project management function as a line item entry (1.2 in Exhibit 5-4) in the WBS. Every other entry includes the labor cost of the tasks. The project manager, though, and any other project office staff spread their labor costs across the entire project. That is, the project manager doesn't just work on a task. She is supervising the entire project. Therefore, rather than try to apportion the project manager's time to every single task, it is much easier to include a separate WBS entry for this function and then provide a total cost for the estimated project duration.

Network Analysis

The WBS provides the basis for development of the *network analysis*, a method of representing the activities or tasks of a project by a series of lines and nodes to show the interrelations of these various activities. Several important pieces of information can be derived from a network analysis: the critical path, which is the path that takes the longest to traverse (the critical path determines the minimum schedule length with a given resource allocation), early start and finish times for each activity, and the amount of slack time the project manager can expect for each activity. (See Chapter 6 for a discussion of how to develop and interpret a network.)

Scheduling

Scheduling the project activities is difficult unless there is a clear understanding of all the activity requirements and how each of the activities relates to the others. For instance, a number of activities cannot begin until one or more preceding activities have been completed. Without a detailed breakdown of the project, it is easy to overlook these interrelationships or to overlook certain activities completely. The WBS is a way to analyze the project's activities from the perspective of creating schedules that will have the requisite beginning and ending points for each while observing their dependency hierarchies.

Project Control

Controlling a project requires a complete understanding of the project activities: who is responsible for each, how they interrelate, how much each element should cost, and how long each activity should take for completion. The WBS is the basis of each of the tools already discussed, which, in turn, are the tools that the project manager uses to track and control the project.

Summary

This chapter has presented a simple approach to the development of a WBS, a powerful tool but one that is not clearly described in the literature. Although WBS development is not easy, following the approach and the guidelines provides a workable model for the project manager. Some important guidelines for WBS development are:

- The project name or contract name is always the first-level entry.
- There will be only one first-level entry for each project.
- The first three levels of a WBS are managerial levels.
- Technical project work usually occurs at the fourth and fifth levels.
- The lowest level of any project is usually the fifth level.
- Major subdivisions do not have to be reduced to the same level.

When the WBS is correctly developed and used, it becomes the basis for planning, scheduling, budgeting, and controlling.

Notes

1. A. B. Badiru, *Project Management in Manufacturing and High Technology Operations* (New York: Wiley, 1988); S. F. Love, *Achieving Problem Free Project Management* (New York: Wiley, 1989).

Additional References of Interest

Frame, J. Davidson. *Managing Projects in Organizations.* Rev. ed. San Francisco: Jossey-Bass, 1995.

Kerzner, Harold. *Project Management: A Systems Approach to Planning, Scheduling, and Controlling.* 5th ed. New York: Van Nostrand Reinhold, 1995.

Knutson, Joan, and Ira Bitz. *Project Management: How to Plan and Manage Successful Projects.* New York: AMACOM, 1991.

Meredith, Jack R., and Samuel J. Mantel, Jr. *Project Management: A Managerial Approach.* 3d ed. New York: Wiley, 1995.

Chapter 6
Network Analysis

Often the parts are not the same as the whole—
look at the entire picture before you act.

—Robin T. Peterson, *Managing Without Blinders*

Prior to 1950, no project tracking or controlling methods adequately showed the interdependencies of project activities. In the 1950s, this all changed when the Project Evaluation Review Technique (PERT) was developed by Lockheed and Booz-Allen and Hamilton as an evaluation and tracking tool for the navy's Polaris missile program. Since then, other network analysis tools have been developed to compensate for shortcomings or disadvantages of the PERT method or to provide specialized capabilities that PERT does not possess. Although there are several network analysis tools available, the three most common ones are the PERT, the critical path method (CPM), and the precedence diagram method (PDM). This chapter discusses each method and demonstrates how each is used to analyze a project.

Logic Diagrams and Networks

A logic diagram shows the major elements of a task and their logical relationship to each other. Exhibit 6-1 shows a logic diagram that describes the process for a man getting dressed and eating breakfast in the morning. The boxes, called *nodes*, depict

Exhibit 6-1. A logic diagram for a man getting dressed and eating breakfast.

(Time in minutes)

the tasks that have to be accomplished, and the arrows, sometimes called *arcs*, show the relationship of the tasks to each other and the sequence in which they have to be accomplished.

There are two ways to construct a network: One shows the activities on the nodes (AON), and the second shows the activities on the arrows (AOA). If the activities are shown on the nodes, then the arrows have no substance; that is, they simply show interdependencies and sequences but have no duration or resources attached to them. And if the activities are shown on the arrows, then the nodes have no substance. They just indicate the beginning or ending points for the activities.

PERT and CPM are both AOA networks. The PDM is an AON analysis method. Neither the AOA nor the AON method is particularly difficult to construct once the basic principles of construction are understood. The analysis of each type is exactly the same. However, the AOA method does have the disadvantage that dummy activities can occur. A *dummy activity* is one that places an additional constraint on one or more activities but has no duration or resources associated with it. For example, suppose task C is *dependent* upon task A for a key design drawing. Task C, then, is constrained by the technical activity of task A, and cannot start until task A is completed. Suppose also that task B is *independent* of both task A and task C. That means task B can begin simultaneously with task A, and task C can begin regardless of when task B is completed. Suppose, though, that you plan to utilize some of the task B team members to accomplish task C. Task C then becomes constrained by task B, but not because of a technical dependency between the two. This relationship (the *dummy activity*) between the two tasks is real, but the "activity" of the relationship requires no actual expenditure of resources, and no work is involved getting from one task to the other. Nevertheless, task C cannot begin until task B is finished. The dummy activity will be completely described and demonstrated in due course, but since this is a characteristic of the AOA-type network and adds a small degree of complexity to the description of it, we shall consider the slightly simpler AON network first. AON networks do not have dummy activities and therefore are somewhat easier to construct.

AON Networks (the Precedence Diagram Method)

AON networks describe a project with the nodes representing the activities or work units. Usually each node represents the lowest level of the WBS so work unit relationships can be assessed. The network can be drawn showing any level of the WBS, however, depending on the level of detail needed and the desired result. For instance, if the project is a fairly long and complex one, it may be useful to do a high-level network analysis to determine the overall schedule and when certain resources might be needed. More detail can be obtained from analyzing the complete project or discrete phases of it. The point is that a network analysis can be performed at various levels of detail over the entire project or over individual tasks, depending on the information needed.

One of the major advantages of the PDM or AON is that it can accommodate different activity sequencing and account for lead and lag. For instance, the AOA method requires that activities be sequenced from the finish of one activity to the start of another. In contrast, the PDM allows the use of finish-to-start, start-to-start, start-to-finish, and finish-to-finish sequencing. Also, the PDM allows the use of lead and lag times if needed. For instance, if one activity is to pour a concrete floor and another is to erect a building frame, the frame can't be built until the concrete floor is dry. So although the concrete floor is poured and that part of the activity is complete, we might need to add a lag time of five days to allow the floor to dry before starting the next activity. The concept of alternative sequencing with lead and lag is shown in Exhibit 6-2.

Basic Network Construction

The WBS is the most important tool of the project manager. From it, all the other tools can be derived. The network is an example of a tool derived from WBS information.

The network is a logic diagram of the interdependencies of the various project tasks. The WBS is an object- or service-ori-

Exhibit 6-2. Alternative task sequencing.

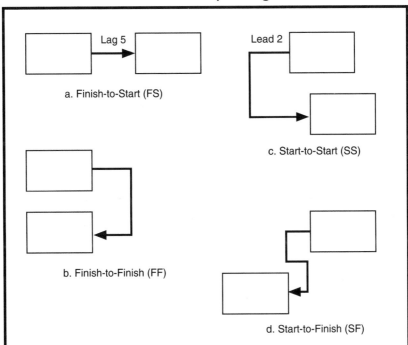

a. Finish-to-Start (FS)

b. Finish-to-Finish (FF)

c. Start-to-Start (SS)

d. Start-to-Finish (SF)

ented depiction of the project with the tasks decomposed into increasingly greater levels of detail until a level is reached to which work can be assigned. This level is called the *work package*.

Once the WBS is developed, three questions have to be answered for each activity in the project in order to construct the network:

1. What activities must be completed before this activity can start? These are the *predecessors*.
2. What activities follow this activity? These are the *successors*.
3. What activities can be accomplished independently or in parallel with this activity?

The first step in constructing a network is to identify every activity and each of its predecessors. The easiest way to do this is to construct a table and, with the help of the project team, analyze the project WBS to determine the predecessors. This analysis which was done for Exhibit 6-1, is recorded in Exhibit 6-3. Exhibit 6-3 also has added estimated duration times for each of the activities and an alphabetic descriptor for each one. The alphabetic descriptor is used instead of the full description of the activity to reduce the clutter on the network. Networks can be complex enough without adding activity descriptions.

Once the predecessors are determined, the network can be drawn as shown in Exhibit 6-4. Some important points to note about the network are that:

- Arrows indicate the direction of the work flow.
- The nodes contain the alphabetic identifier and the duration.
- Every node has either a successor or a predecessor or both, except the beginning and ending ones.

Exhibit 6-3. Analysis of getting dressed and eating breakfast.

Activity	Alphabetic Designator	Immediate Predecessor(s)	Activity Duration (in minutes)
Awake.	a	--	0
Shower.	b	a	10
Shave.	c	b	5
Dress.	d	c	15
Start coffee.	e	d	2
Walk dog.	f	d	6
Retrieve newspaper.	g	f	1
Start toast.	h	g	2
Boil eggs.	i	g	3
Set table.	j	g	3
Serve breakfast.	k	h, i, j	2
Eat breakfast.	l	k	15
Read newspaper.	m	k	15
Leave for work.	n	l, m	0

Exhibit 6-4. AON (precedence diagram) for getting dressed and eating breakfast.

(Time in minutes)

- It is not necessary to draw a dummy activity to describe the project.

AOA Network (The PERT Method)

Activity-on-the-arrow construction follows the same general procedure as the AON in that the initial steps are to construct the table shown in Exhibit 6-5. An additional constraint in the construction of an AOA network is necessary, however: Each activity must be represented by its own arrow, and only one arrow can be drawn between the same two nodes. This situation gives rise to the possibility of a dummy activity. Exhibit 6-5 demonstrates how to construct a dummy activity when two activities occur between the same two nodes or when a nontechnical dependency exists between the two.

In Exhibit 6-5A, two activities, a and b, emanate from node 1, and both terminate at node 2. However, the rule of network construction is that only one arrow can be drawn between the same two nodes. To avoid this situation, a third node, node 3, is drawn as the terminus of activity b. Then a dummy activity is drawn from node 3 to node 2. The dummy activity is always shown as a dashed line to distinguish it from normal project activities. Another important characteristic of the dummy activity is that it has no substance; that is, no resources and no dura-

Exhibit 6-5. Constructing dummy activities.

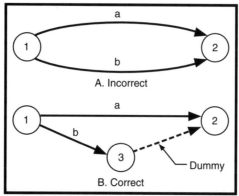

tion are assigned to it. The dummy construction is simply a way of indicating an additional constraint that has to be met prior to any activity beginning at node 2.

The numbers within the nodes of an AON network have no significance other than to identify the node. It is a convenient way of keeping track of activities in the network. The order of numbering the nodes is generally unimportant. However, the convention is to number them beginning at the left of the network (the start) and progressing to the end. In the event of parallel activities, the nodes are usually numbered from the top to the bottom.

The network for the getting-dressed example as it is drawn in the AOA format is shown in Exhibit 6-6. Notice the differences between Exhibits 6-4 and 6-6. Although the two networks look similar, there are some distinct differences. First, the duration times and the activity designators are written on the arrows of Exhibit 6-6 and the nodes of Exhibit 6-4. But, most important in the AOA network, there has to be a dummy activity drawn from nodes 8 and 9 to node 10, and from nodes 12 and 13 to node 14 to show the additional constraint on activity g. We did not have to indicate a dummy in Exhibit 6-4 since arrows in the AON networks only show sequences and constraints and have no substance. Since the arrows in an AOA network have values associated with them, we had to invent the dummy activity. Remember that the dummy itself has no duration, resources, or anything else associated with it. It just shows the added constraint that activity g cannot begin before activities d and f are finished.

Estimating Activity Duration

One of the big challenges in constructing a network is estimating activity duration. If a project is very similar to numerous other previous projects in the company, then duration can be estimated with good accuracy from experience and historical data. In the construction industry, for example, the various phases in building a house can be predicted with great accuracy. When the project manager approaches individuals responsible for each

Exhibit 6-6. AOA Network of getting dressed and eating breakfast.

(Time in minutes)

task, they can readily assign a duration. What happens, though, in a research and development project where the project is breaking new ground and is completely new to the company? How can the project manager estimate duration and account for the risk associated with the uncertainty in a project?

It was this problem that led to the development of PERT. The Polaris missile program was so complex and there was so much new technology associated with it that a new tool for analyzing the project had to be developed. A key difference in the PERT analysis from other network analysis methods is that the duration of each activity is statistically derived. That is, each activity duration is determined using three times: the most optimistic estimate, the most pessimistic estimate, and the most likely estimate. Then applying the formula:

$$T_e = \frac{a + 4m + b}{6}$$

where:

a = most optimistic time
b = most pessimistic time
m = most likely time
T_e = estimate duration

the duration time, T_e, is calculated. An example of this process is shown in Exhibit 6-7.

T_e for the first activity, system design, is calculated by using the formula above. Substituting the values for a, b, and m, we get:

$$T_e = \frac{6 + (4 \times 8.25) + 9}{6}$$

$$= \frac{48}{6}$$

$$= 8 \text{ weeks}$$

The T_e for all subsequent activities is calculated in the same way. It is the T_e value that is used as the duration time on the activity arrows in the PERT network.

The PERT formula describes the beta distribution, or the

Exhibit 6-7. Estimated durations using PERT analysis.

Activity	Optimistic Times (weeks)	Most Likely Times (weeks)	Pessimistic Times (weeks)	T_e
System design	6	8.25	9	8
Procure hardware components	4	4.75	7	5
Assemble system	2	5.5	6	5
Test hardware system	2	2	2	2
Develop software	10	13.25	15	13
Test software	3	4	5	4
Integrate hardware and software	2	3.75	7	4
Test integrated system	2	3	4	3
Deliver system	1	1	1	1
Install system	2	2	2	2

well-known bell curve, shown in Exhibit 6-8. Most of us are very familiar with the bell curve and know that statistically approximately 68 percent of the samples of a population will fall between -1σ and $+1\sigma$, where σ represents the standard deviation. Similarily, approximately 95 percent of the sampled data will fall between -2σ and $+2\sigma$, and a little over 99 percent will fall between -3σ and $+3\sigma$. What many people do *not* realize is that the area under the beta distribution curve from -3σ to $+1\sigma$ contains 85 percent of the samples, from -3σ to $+2\sigma$ contains 99 percent, and from -3σ to $+3\sigma$ contains nearly 100 percent of the samples.

Given that the formula for T_e is actually an average number, the duration calculated from the formula is the mean of the bell curve, or at the 50 percent mark. Hence, there is only a 50 percent probability that a task can be finished before or on the T_e calculated by the PERT formula. In order to have an 85 percent chance of completing the task on or before T_e, the duration time has to be increased by one standard deviation; a 99 percent probability requires increasing the T_e by two standard deviations, and so on.

Exhibit 6-8. The bell curve and standard deviation.

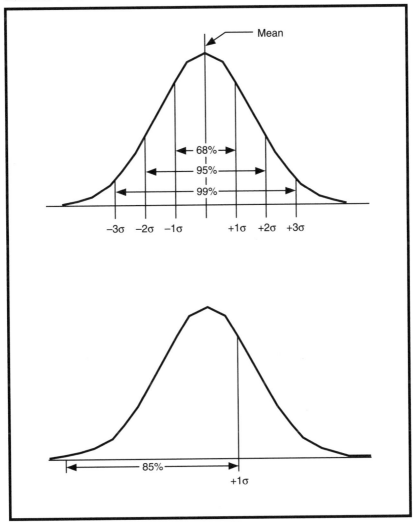

Standard deviation is not difficult to calculate. The optimistic and pessimistic times used for the T_e calculation are also used to calculate standard deviation where standard deviation, σ, is given by:

$$\sigma = \frac{b - a}{6}$$

where:

   b = pessimistic time
   a = optimistic time

Hence, for our example from Exhibit 6-7, the standard deviation for the system design activity is:

$$\sigma = \frac{9 - 6}{6}$$

$$= .5$$

Therefore, to ensure that we have a 100 percent probability of finishing the system design activity on time, we must add 3 σs to the calculated T_e. Hence, the duration time for this activity then becomes:

$$T_e = 8.83 + 3 \times \sigma$$

$$= 8.83 + (3 \times .5)$$

$$= 8.83 + 1.5$$

$$= 10.33 \text{ weeks}$$

The beauty of the PERT analysis is that it provides a way to account for risk in duration or schedule estimation.

Most project managers do not calculate standard deviations for every activity, although I recommend it. Instead, they calculate the standard deviations of the activities on the critical path and apply those to determine the overall schedule duration.

Calculating the Critical Path and the Project Duration

The critical path in a network is defined as the longest path from the beginning of the network to the end. A path is a track defined by following the arrows from node to node, from network start to network finish, in the direction of the arrows. Suppose we have the project described by Exhibit 6-9. Using these dura-

Exhibit 6-9. PERT durations for a generic project.

Activity	Predecessor(s)	Times (days)			
		a	m	b	T_e
a	--	6	7.5	9	7.5
b	a	4	5.0	6	5.0
c	a	2	5.5	6	5.0
d	a	10	14.75	15	14.0
e	b	3	4.0	5	4.0
f	c, d	2	2.75	5	3.0
g	d	5	6.0	7	6.0
h	e, f, g	4	5.75	9	6.0

tion times for the activities and their predecessors, we can construct the PERT network diagram shown in Exhibit 6-10. The various paths in this project are indicated on the exhibit.

In order to determine the critical path for the network in Exhibit 6-10, we calculate the earliest occurrence time (EOT) at each of the nodes. The EOT is the earliest time that a succeeding activity can start. Looking at Exhibit 6-10, we see that the earliest that activities b, c, and d can start is at the end of 7.5 days because it takes 7.5 days to accomplish the work of activity a. The earliest that activity e can begin is at the end of 12.5 days (start of activity b is at 8.5 days and it takes 5 days to accomplish the activity). The process continues in this fashion to the end of the network. However, notice at node 6 that there will be four EOT possibilities coming into node 6. If we look at the path a-b-e, the EOT at node 6 will be 16.5 days; path a-c-f yields an EOT of 15.5 days; path a-d-dummy-f yields an EOT of 24.5 days; and, path a-d-g yields an EOT of 28.5 days. The correct EOT to use is 28.5 days because the rule is that all activities have to be completed before the following activity or activities can begin.

Hence, if we choose any EOT of less duration than 28.5 days, one or more of the other activities could not be completed. With the EOT at node 6 being 28.5 days, to get to node 8 will require 33.5 days. This number, 33.5 days, is the estimated average duration required to accomplish this project. Remember that

Exhibit 6-10. Paths of a network.

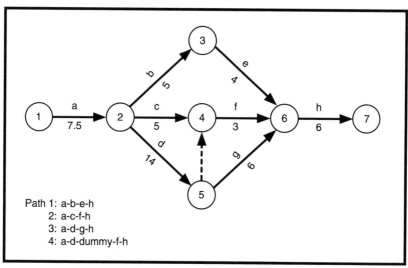

Path 1: a-b-e-h
   2: a-c-f-h
   3: a-d-g-h
   4: a-d-dummy-f-h

there is only a 50 percent probability of completing the project within 33.5 days. To ensure a 100 percent probability of success, we have to calculate the standard deviations of the activities along the critical path. But first we have to determine which is the critical path.

Determining the Critical Path

The critical path is defined as the longest path traversing the network from the beginning to the end. In our example, the longest path is a-d-g-h. It takes longer to do the activities of that path than any of the others. Hence, the critical path is a-d-g-h. To determine the standard deviations of each of these activities, we refer to Exhibit 6-9 and use the optimistic and pessimistic values of each of the activities. For activity a, the most optimistic time is 6 days and the most pessimistic time is 9 days. Using our formula for σ, we can calculate the standard deviation for activity a:

$$\sigma = \frac{b - a}{6}$$

$$= \frac{9 - 6}{6}$$

$$= .5$$

In like manner, we calculate the standard deviations for activities d, g, and h, to get the values .83, .33, and .33, respectively. The standard deviation for the critical path, then, is the total of these four σs:

$$\sigma \text{ critical path} = .50 + .83 + .33 + .33$$

$$= 1.99 \text{ days}$$

The schedule length for our example project, for a 100 percent probability of completion, becomes:

$$T_e = 33.5 + (3 \times \sigma)$$

$$= 33.5 + (3 \times 1.99)$$

$$= 33.5 + 5.97$$

$$= 39.5 \text{ days}$$

Slack or Float in a Project

One of the primary uses of a network analysis is to determine how much slack (or float; generally the terms are used interchangeably) is available in the project. *Slack* refers to the amount of extra time available between the end of one activity and the beginning of the succeeding one(s). It is not the same as lead or lag time. Slack results because the activities on noncritical paths finish sooner than those on the critical path, and therefore there is some extra time available before a succeeding activity can begin. *Lead* or *lag time*, on the other hand, is time built into the schedule to control the start and end times of activities.

Slack is important to the project manager because it allows leeway in starting times of certain activities so that the use of resources can be optimized. That is, if there are fewer personnel available to work on the project than are needed, then it may be possible to do the job anyway if some of the activities can be delayed so that the total number of people needed is equal to or below the number available. This is called *resource leveling*. This schedule optimization can be accomplished only if there is some slack available in the project. We determine the amount of slack in a project by calculating the early start, early finish, late start, and late finish of each project. We already calculated the early finish (EF) for each of the activities of the example in Exhibit 6-10 when we calculated the EOT. The EF or EOT of the longest path will determine the schedule duration. Using the same example, Exhibit 6-10, let us calculate the other three values.

Calculating Early Start/Early Finish

The early start (ES) and early finish (EF) values are determined by starting from the first node. We have already determined these values, and they are shown in Exhibit 6-11. The early start for activity a is 0. Starting at 0, the earliest that activity a can end is 7.5 days since it takes 7.5 days to accomplish the activity. The earliest that activities b, c, and d can start is 7.5 days. Notice that the ES of succeeding activities will be the EF of the previous activity except where several activities feed into the same node, as into node 6. In this case, the ES for activity h will be the *larger* of the EF numbers feeding into the node.

Calculating Late Start/Late Finish

Calculating the late start (LS) and late finish (LF) numbers is done in the reverse order, from the end of the network to the beginning. This is so because we start with the schedule duration, found by determining the EF of the critical path, and work backward. Exhibit 6-12 shows the completed network analysis with all the times filled in. Note that the latest the project can finish is 33.5 days (we can use the estimated time, T_e, for this part of the analysis because the relative activity durations will yield the correct slack in the activity). The latest that activity h can finish, then, is 33.5 days. The latest that activity h can start is 27.5

Exhibit 6-11. Early start and early finish times.

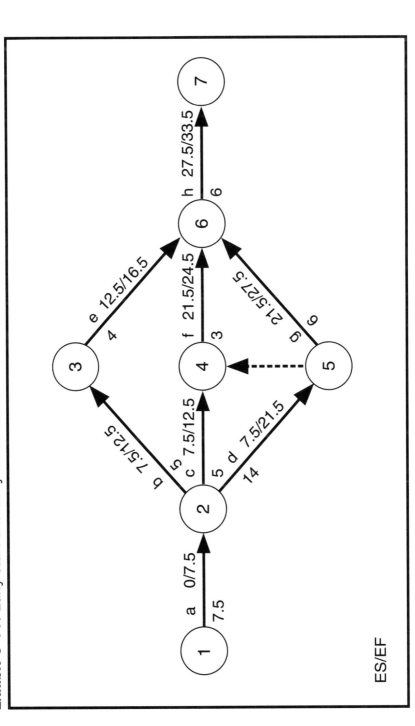

ES/EF

Exhibit 6-12. Early start, early finish, late start, and late finish times.

ES/EF
LS/LF

days since it takes 6 days to accomplish the activity. The latest that activities e, f, and g can finish will have to be the LS time of activity h since each has to be finished in time for h to start. This process is continued backward through the network until the beginning is reached.

Notice what happens at node 2. We have a decision to make about which is the correct LF number for activity a since we have three choices coming into node 2. This time the correct number is the smaller of the choices. (Going forward through the network from beginning to end, the early finish is the larger number when there are several choices entering a single node; going backward through the network from the end to the beginning, the late start is the smaller number when there are several choices exiting a single node.)

Slack in an activity is calculated by subtracting its early finish from the late finish or the early start from the late start of the activity. For instance, looking at Exhibit 6-12, the slack in activity b is 11 days. We can find the slack in the other activities in the same manner, that is, subtracting EF from LF. But notice that activities a, d, g, and h have zero slack. This is a second important characteristic of the critical path; the first characteristic is that the critical path is the longest path in the network, and the second is that none of the activities on the critical path has any slack. The zero slack is the reason that the critical path is called "critical." With zero slack available, any delay in any of the activities on the critical path will cause the project to miss its scheduled finish time. In essence, then, the project manager's focus is on managing the critical path activities.

Perhaps a few words to clarify critical activity or task are in order. In discussions about critical tasks, many who are new to the concept invariably assume that to have a critical task automatically means that there are also noncritical, in the sense of unimportant or less important, tasks. *There are no unimportant tasks; all tasks are critical in the sense they are necessary for the completion of the project.* However, that is not the way we are using the term *critical task* or *critical path*. By critical task I mean that it is a task that has zero slack and is on the path that defines the schedule. Hence, the task is critical because it directly affects the schedule if there is delay in it.

The Precedence Diagramming Method

The PDM is the preferred network analysis method because it follows a logic diagram that is easier to visualize and construct, and it avoids the need for dummy activities. Project management software programs base their network analyses on the PDM because the dummy activities of the PERT method are not easy to model. (Microsoft Project™ calls its network view "PERT." However, it does not accommodate a statistical determination of duration, characteristic of the PERT method; it draws the tasks or activities as AON, and the final network view is a classic PDM network.)

The analysis of the PDM is the same as in PERT once the duration estimates are known. That is, early and late start, early and late finish, schedule length, and critical path are determined the same way in both methods. The difference is that in the PDM there are no dummy activities, and the activity information is presented on the nodes. To illustrate this difference, Exhibit 6-13 is the PDM view of the previous PERT analysis shown in Exhibit 6-12, the generic project example.

One final point needs to be made about PDM. Occasionally, you will not have an accurate duration estimate for one or more of the tasks in a project. You simply use the PERT method to determine the duration estimates for these tasks, and remember to apply a standard deviation for your estimate.

The Critical Path Method

The CPM is very similar to PERT, except that the duration times are not statistically determined. That means that the duration times for the activities of a project are known with a high degree of accuracy, usually because of past experience and historical data on similar projects.

The CPM method is used almost exclusively by the construction industry, and often by other industries as long as the project is straightforward and durations can be estimated with

Exhibit 6-13. PDM view of the specific project.

a high degree of accuracy. In the case of the CPM, only one time is used for each estimated duration.

The CPM is an AOA network, so it looks exactly like the PERT network, and the analysis process is exactly the same. The major use of the CPM, though, is as a cost-estimating tool. The CPM is used to *crash the schedule,* which is a way of compressing the schedule. The reason this becomes a cost-estimating tool is that compressing the schedule usually requires adding resources, which adds costs to the project. Additional costs can be acceptable in a project provided that the benefits of crashing the schedule offset these costs. At some point, the costs become prohibitive, and crashing the schedule is no longer a viable option.

Crashing the schedule is accomplished by examining the activities on the critical path to determine if any of them can be shortened, by either increasing the resources or doing some of the activity's subtasks in parallel. The process is to reduce one or more of the activities on the critical path by one time unit. For instance, if the duration units are days, then the critical path should be reduced by one day and the impact assessed. This process should continue until the desired result is achieved, a point is reached beyond which the costs are unacceptable, or the critical path is reduced to a point beyond which a new critical path is created.

Clearly it is of no benefit to add resources to activities that are not on the critical path because to do so would add costs with no attendant benefits in schedule.

Summary

One major tool for project managers is the network analysis. The three most common network analysis tools are the PERT, CPM, and PDM. The PERT is the only network tool that explicitly accounts for risk in schedule estimating. One of the disadvantages of both the PERT and the CPM is that there can be a potential for a dummy activity. Although the dummy is not hard to account for, it is an additional constraint that is not required in the PDM. Finally, one of the major advantages of the PDM is that alternative sequencing between activities is possible as well as the use of lead and lag. Neither the PERT nor the CPM allows anything but finish-to-start sequencing in the activity relationships, and lead and lag cannot be shown discretely in these methods. Lead and lag can be accommodated by PERT and CPM, but only by adding them to the individual task durations. Of course, doing so complicates project progress tracking.

Additional References of Interest

Kerzner, Harold. *Project Management: A Systems Approach to Planning, Scheduling, and Controlling.* 5th ed. New York: Van Nostrand Reinhold, 1995.

Meredith, Jack R., and Samuel J. Mantel, Jr. *Project Management: A Managerial Approach.* New York: Wiley, 1995.

Nicholas, John M. *Managing Business and Engineering Projects: Concepts and Implementation:* Englewood Cliffs, N.J.: Prentice-Hall, 1990.

Chapter 7
Earned Value

Given for one instant an intelligence . . . if . . . this intelligence were vast enough to submit these data to analysis, . . . to it nothing would be uncertain, and the future as the past would be present to its eyes.

—Pierre Simon de Laplace

Prior to the 1960s, tracking project progress essentially consisted of monitoring the actual costs against the budget and the actual schedule against the estimate, but no method was available that assessed the combined impacts of costs and schedule. Nor were there any standards for analyzing and reporting these data. This problem came to a head in the Department of Defense (DOD) because of the size and complexity of its projects. The problem was exacerbated by having multiple contractors working on the same project and all having their own tracking and reporting systems.

In the 1960s, with the U.S. Air Force taking the lead, the DOD set about to develop a DOD instruction, identified in governmental jargon as a DODI, that would provide guidance to contractors for:

- Developing work breakdown structures.
- Developing certain key planning elements such as baselines.
- Defining cost allocations and procedures for collecting and reporting cost data.

- Analyzing budget and schedule variances and predicting future project costs.
- Preparing performance reports.

The first instruction, DODI 7000.2, was implemented in 1967. It took some time before DOD contractors fully embraced DODI 7000.2 because it required some radical changes in their accounting systems. The DOD allowed a period of transition but made it clear that to be awarded a DOD contract, the contractor had to abide by the requirements of DODI 7000.2. By the early 1970s, all DOD contractors had fully implemented the procedures required by the instruction.

The DODI 7000.2 has remained essentially unchanged since it was written. It was superseded by DODI 5000.2 in 1991, with the primary change being a supplemental user guide, but with little else changing. This instruction is also known as the cost schedule control system criteria (C/SCSC).

One of the most beneficial components of the C/SCSC is the method of project progress analysis known as earned value. This method was exclusively used by the DOD and its contractors until the late 1980s or early 1990s, when the private sector began to adopt it as the analysis tool of choice. The method can be used on small and large projects and is independent of the type of contract executing the project.

The Earned Value Concept

The concept of earned value is sometimes difficult to grasp, though not because the concept or the procedure is difficult. (On the contrary, the procedure is very straightforward.) The problem is basically twofold: Earned value has a language of its own, and schedule is measured in terms of dollars instead of time. Since measuring schedule in this fashion goes against intuition and experience, some people focus on the language rather than on the concepts of earned value. The result is that learning the earned value analysis technique is harder than it should be.

The key to understanding earned value is in understanding three terms:

1. Budgeted cost of work scheduled (BCWS)
2. Actual cost of work performed (ACWP)
3. Budgeted cost of work performed (BCWP; also known as *earned value,* hence the origin of the term for this technique)

Once you have mastered these terms and the concepts they represent, all the other terms and components of an earned value analysis are easy to remember and use.

Budgeted Cost of Work Scheduled

The BCWS is the project budget, or what is expected to be spent to accomplish the project objectives. This meaning of this term is not very different from our usual understanding. The project manager gets the components of BCWS from the WBS and constructs a cumulative, time-phased graph showing the anticipated budget from the start of the project to the end. This budget line is the standard against which the project expenditures are measured, bringing us to the next definition of interest, ACWP.

Actual Cost of Work Performed

ACWP too is a very familiar concept. The ACWP is what it costs to do the project. In other words, ACWP is what is actually spent in performing the tasks of the project.

Prior to the development of the earned value analysis technique, the BCWS and the ACWP were used to analyze project progress by a comparison of budget and actual expenditures. The problem is that this type of analysis does not account for the impact of schedule variances, at least not in any way that is obvious or interpretable. For instance, at the end of month 6, the ACWP might be higher than the budget for that period. On the surface, this would indicate that the project was overspending its budget. However, it might be that one or more of the tasks were started and completed earlier than planned so that more money was expended but more work was accomplished. This problem led to the next term, the BCWP, or earned value.

Budgeted Cost of Work Performed

The BCWP element of the earned value analysis is the term and concept that is different from how we usually view schedule tracking. The C/SCSC developed a method for tracking schedule in terms of dollars earned for the actual amount of work accomplished, or BCWP. People new to the concept of earned value often have trouble separating this term from the actual cost of the task or project, but there is a significant difference between the ACWP and the BCWP. The ACWP represents the amount of money *actually spent* on the work completed; the BCWP is the amount of money *budgeted* for the work that has been completed.

To explain the concept of BCWP, we will start with the *fifty-fifty rule*, a widely accepted method for determining how much work has been completed at any analysis point in the project. The rule was adopted as a way to estimate how much work has been completed on a task or project. Suppose there is a contract to manufacture 100 desk chairs, and they are to be delivered in four weeks. If the project manager's schedule is to produce 25 chairs per week, then it is not difficult to determine whether the project is ahead or behind schedule when the newly manufactured chairs are counted at the end of every week. However, if the project is to develop software or is some type of services effort, then determining what percentage of the work has been accomplished at random times in the project's life is difficult, if not impossible. Hence the development of the fifty-fifty rule.

The fifty-fifty rule assumes that when a task begins, it is 50 percent complete; when the task is completed, it is 100 percent complete. The reason for this assumption is to provide a consistent means of estimating how much of the planned work was accomplished—that is, BCWP—at any point in the task. This method is so widely accepted that a contractor has to justify using any other method before a customer will approve it. But there is an obvious problem with the fifty-fifty rule. If a project status is taken immediately after a task begins, then the project manager can take credit for finishing 50 percent of the task's work virtually before it even begins. And if the status is taken near the end of the task, the project team may be actually 90 percent complete but can take credit for only half of it. Exhibit 7-1 more clearly depicts the fifty-fifty rule.

There are four tasks shown in the exhibit, and, for the sake of simplicity, we have estimated the budget of each to be $1,000. From the exhibit, we can see that Task 1 began on time and finished on time. Since we budgeted Task 1 to cost $1,000, we can take full credit for it. Task 2 started on time and was completed early. Therefore, we can take full credit, or $1,000, for this task. Task 3 was supposed to have started but has not, so we get no credit for the task. Task 4 started late but hasn't been completed,

Exhibit 7-1. Determining BCWP by the fifty-fifty rule.

so we get 50 percent credit, or $500, for starting the task. To summarize, the BCWP for these tasks is:

Task 1	$1,000
Task 2	1,000
Task 3	0
Task 4	500
	$2,500

The BCWP for these four tasks is $2,500. We also know what the budgeted cost of work schedule (BCWS) is. Since we budgeted $1,000 for each of the tasks, the BCWS is $4,000. (If the dotted line in Exhibit 7-1 had cut through any of the planned boxes, we would use the fifty-fifty rule to determine the percentage to apply to determine BCWS as we did for the BCWP.)

Notice that I have said nothing about the actual cost of the work to this point. Suppose the expenditures for Task 1 were $1,000—right on budget. But Task 2 didn't take as long as anticipated so we spent less, say, $800. Task 3 hasn't started yet, so nothing has been spent on it. Now suppose we have spent $600 to date on Task 4. Summarizing actual costs, we have:

Task 1	$1,000
Task 2	800
Task 3	0
Task 4	600
	$2,400

Therefore, the BCWS = $4,000, ACWP = $2,400, and BCWP = $2,500 for this particular time in the project's life cycle. So what do these numbers tell us?

If BCWP is the amount earned and ACWP is the amount spent, it is clear that we are spending at a slower rate than we are earning (BCWP − ACWP = 2,500 − 2,400 = 100). Hence, the project is under budget by $100. But if BCWP is the amount earned and BCWS is the amount scheduled to spend, then clearly we are behind schedule (BCWP − BCWS = 2,500 − 4,000 = −1,500). Remember that we have converted schedule to a dollar basis. Hence, we interpret the negative result as showing that we have not earned as much as we had scheduled to be earned.

Because some organizations, or some customers, are more conservative than the fifty-fifty rule will accommodate, other methods for estimating percentage of work completion are used. For instance, some organizations use a 20 percent credit for beginning a task and 80 percent at completion; others are more conservative and give no credit for starting a task and 100 percent credit only when it is completed. Even so, the fifty-fifty rule is by far the most common method for estimating percentage of task completion when it is not possible to determine the actual amount of work completed.

Evaluating Project Status

The rationale of earned value can be represented by some easy-to-remember formulas. Comparing the amount earned in a project to the amount spent is what we call *cost variance* and is represented by the formula:

$$CV = BCWP - ACWP$$

The comparison of BCWP to BCWS is called *schedule variance,* and it is represented by the formula:

$$SV = BCWP - BCWS$$

I have worked out a simple method for remembering these two formulas. First, notice that the first term—BCWP, or the earned value term—is the same in both formulas. Since we are doing an earned value analysis, it should not be hard to remember to start with the "earned value" term. Now, let us examine the two equations, the one for cost variance first:

$$CV = BC\underline{WP} - AC\underline{WP}$$

Notice that the last two letters of these two terms are the same. Note as well that the first two letters of each of these terms deal with costs (budgeted cost and actual cost), and the last two letters deal with schedule (work performed); since WP is the same in both formulas, then we are holding the schedule constant while determining how the cost varies.

Now look at the equation for schedule variance:

$$SV = \underline{BC}WP - \underline{BC}WS$$

In this formula, the first two letters, budgeted cost, are the same. Hence, we can argue that we are holding the cost constant while determining how the schedule varies.

Looking at these equations in this way should provide a means of deriving them without having to memorize them or worry about whether the terms are in the right place.

In the example, I alluded to the fact that negative numbers indicate that the project is over budget or behind schedule. Not surprisingly, then, positive numbers indicate that the project is under budget and ahead of schedule. Zero for CV or SV indicates that the project is on budget or on schedule.

Performance Indexes

It is often more meaningful to have some percentage measurement or index of how the project is doing. The two most often used indexes are the cost performance index (CPI) and the schedule performance index (SPI). The same terms are used for each of these as were used to determine CV and SV, respectively, except that instead of subtracting the terms, we divide them. Hence, we have:

$$CPI = \frac{BCWP}{ACWP}$$

and

$$SPI = \frac{BCWP}{BCWS}$$

David Frame refers to the CPI as the "burn rate," or the rate at which we are spending money, and this is a very good way to look at it.[1] Another way of looking at CPI and SPI is as efficiency rates. For example, using the previous example where BCWP = 2,000 and ACWP = 2,400, the CPI is:

$$\frac{2,500}{2,400} = 1.04$$

This means that we are "burning" money more slowly than we are making it. Looking at it as an efficiency rate, we are making four cents for every dollar being spent.

The SPI can be analyzed in the same way. Again, using the previous example, the BCWP = 2,000 and BCWS = 4,000. The SPI becomes:

$$\frac{2,500}{4,000} = .63$$

Hence, we have accomplished only a little over half the work that was scheduled; the job is only 63 percent complete.

Estimate at Completion and Estimate to Complete

Two important terms—estimate at completion (EAC) and estimate to complete (ETC)—sound a lot alike but yield different, although related, information.

Estimate at completion is the estimated final cost of the project. A new EAC is determined as the project progresses and more information is available to the project manager relative to how realistic the original budget and schedule estimates were. Also, unexpected events will occur that positively or negatively affect the project, thus making the original estimated total cost of the project wrong.

The *estimate to complete* is the estimate of the amount of money required to finish the project from the point that a progress analysis is made to the end of the project. In short, EAC is the difference between the new estimate at completion and the amount of money actually spent to date.

Estimate at Completion

It is important to keep a running tab of the total cost of the project. At the beginning of the project, the project team will have determined a budget, called the *budget at completion* (BAC). Depending on how the project is progressing, the original budget might not hold up. Therefore, every time the project manager takes a snapshot in time to determine how the project is doing, one of the key elements of the analysis is a new estimate at completion (EAC), calculated as:

$$EAC = \frac{BAC}{CPI}$$

Suppose that the total project's budget at completion was $100,000. With our CPI of 1.04, the new estimate at completion, at our current rate of performance, would be:

$$EAC = \frac{100,000}{1.04}$$
$$= \$96,153.85$$

Hence, at this point in the project's life cycle, we are doing better than our original total budget estimate. At the current rate, the project will cost only a little over $96,000, almost $4,000 less than the original estimate.

Estimate to Complete

Once the new estimate at completion has been determined, the final key element of the earned value analysis can be calculated: the estimate to complete or the amount of money needed to complete the project from this point. The EAC is calculated by:

$$EAC = ETC - ACWP$$

In the example, the ETC is $96,154, and the ACWP is $2,400. Therefore, our new estimate to complete the project is:

$$EAC = 96,154 - 2,400$$
$$= \$93,754$$

Exhibit 7-2 explains the various elements of the earned value analysis and shows the relationship of each.

Exhibit 7-2. Elements of the earned value analysis.

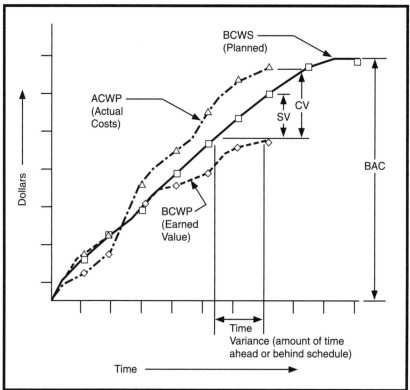

Summary

The earned value analysis technique was developed by the Department of Defense when it became obvious that a standard method was needed to track, analyze, and report project progress. The result was a DOD instruction that defines cost and schedule criteria, known as the cost/schedule control system criteria (C/SCSC). One of the most important tools to come out of the DODI is the earned value technique, which explicitly accounts for schedule impacts by identifying a way to associate schedule with percentage of work completed, or "earned."

Although the earned value method was developed by the

DOD to be used by defense contractors, the method has been discovered by the private sector as well. It is now widely used for tracking and analyzing project progress not only because it is the most accurate method developed to date, but because it can be used effectively with both small and large projects. In addition, the earned value concept is contract independent. That is, regardless of whether the contact is a fixed-fee or cost-plus type of contract, an earned value analysis is equally usable and effective.

Note

1. J. Davidson Frame, *The New Project Management* (San Francisco: Jossey-Bass, 1994).

Part Two
Managing a Project

Introduction to Part Two

In Part One, I discussed the various human and technical skills and tools needed for project management. In Part Two, you will learn where and when to apply this knowledge.

A project has a life cycle with several phases, much the same as a human: It starts slowly in the concept and development phases, builds during development to a peak in the implementation phase, and then begins a steady decline until termination. It is often difficult to differentiate between a project's life cycle phases because some overlapping of activities or tasks is inevitable. Even so, it is useful to think in terms of discrete life cycle phases because that facilitates identification of typical project management activities and the associated skills and tools to accomplish them. Exhibit I-1 depicts a typical project having four phases: concept, development, implementation, and termination. The usual activities for each phase are listed along with the tools most often used. Note that the human characteristics and skills of communication, negotiation, leadership, team building, and coping extend across every phase.

The Part Two chapters follow the sequence of a project's life so that the process of managing a project will be clearly defined. By the end of the book, you will have a good understanding of what activities are likely to occur in each phase, what your action should be, and which tools and skills you should use in formulating your response to the activity.

Exhibit I-1. The life cycle of a project, project activities, and required project management skills.

THE PROJECT LIFE CYCLE

Concept	Development	Implementation	Termination
Activities	**Activities**	**Activities**	**Activities**
• Gather data.	• Appoint core team.	• Set up project organization.	• Review and accept project.
• Identify requirements.	• Write project plan.	• Establish detailed requirements.	• Transfer responsibility.
• Develop alternatives	• Develop scope baseline.	• Set up and execute work packages.	• Document and evaluate results.
• Estimate resources.	• Obtain approval to proceed.	• Direct, monitor, and control project.	• Release and redirect resources.
• Develop charter.	• Develop Network analysis.		
	• Kick off project.		
Tools	**Tools**	**Tools**	**Tools**
• Contract, specifications, statement of work (SOW)	• Project management plan	• WBS	• Management plan
• Work Breakdown Structure (WBS)	• WBS	• Gantt chart	• WBS
	• Gantt chart	• Earned value	• Technical/financial audits
	• PERT/CPM	• Reports	• Reports

Human Skills Required

Communications
Negotiation
Leadership
Team-Building
Coping

Chapter 8
Project and Project Manager Selection

It is not enough to appoint project managers; hand them the ball, and tell them to run with it.
—Linn C. Stuckenbruck, then-Professor,
University of Southern California

All projects have a genesis, a starting point. There is a process in every organization that gets projects on the active list; that is, it determines which of the several opportunities the organization will fund or support through the competition cycle. How do these projects get started? What are the criteria for choosing one project over another, for deciding which project offers a greater opportunity for the organization than another does? After the project is chosen, how is the project manager selected? This chapter looks at these questions and provides a clear understanding of how these processes work.

Choosing the Project and Getting Organizational Commitment

In most companies, it is very likely that the project managers are not involved in the project selection process at all. The new-business and marketing staff typically identify potential projects and then "sell" the senior management on the importance of the individual project to the organization. It is only after the project makes the list of business opportunities that a project manager is selected and assigned to the project. There are exceptions, however; the project manager might find herself in the position of participating in the selection process. Not only that, but many companies do not have any identifiable process for selecting projects; they simply go after any contract that seems to have some similarity to previous work done. For both reasons, a clear understanding of how projects are started and how they can be selected and prioritized can be beneficial.

Selection Model Criteria

Basically, there are two types of selection models: nonnumeric and numeric. Organizations that use models to help in the selection and prioritization of projects often use a combination of the two types, but the use of models runs the gambit from "gut feel" to highly sophisticated mathematical simulations.

Models, whether nonnumeric or numeric, should have certain characteristics. Following are the basic criteria, from a study by A. F. Helin and W. E. Souder[1] of the University of Alabama:

1. *Realistic.* There are any number of projects that could benefit the organization. However, if a model, or user of the model, does not take into consideration the technical and cost risks, capital outlay for facilities, and people resources, then any project selected with the model would not reflect a realistic choice.

2. *Capable.* Projects tend to be complex, particularly if they involve high technology or a large engineering or construction effort. Therefore, the model used has to be sophisticated enough to handle multiple-task, multiyear simulations. Otherwise the project cannot be accurately simulated.

3. *Flexible.* Flexibility in a model may be its most important characteristic. Given the complexity of most projects, numerous iterations and what-if scenarios are needed before a prediction of a project's worth to the organization can be made. Further-

more, the project will undoubtedly undergo numerous changes during its lifetime, requiring new evaluations of the project and project status against the organization's strategic business plan. The model must be flexible enough to handle these evaluations.

4. *Ease of use.* A major disadvantage of many numeric models is that they require specialized knowledge or sophisticated computer programming to use them. Consequently, many otherwise very accurate models are not used. Any model should be simple enough to use that any participants in the process can quickly and effectively input required data and extract useable information. Most nonnumeric, and in many cases numeric, models can be set up to use standard software. For instance, most models can be programmed into any of the good spreadsheets such as Lotus 1-2-3 or Quattro-Pro. Also, the common databases, such as d-Base, Access, and Fox Pro, are of benefit in structuring selection models. So even if the model itself is difficult to use, it can usually be programmed in such a way that the user has only to input the data, and the program will make the requisite calculations and provide a translatable readout.

5. *Cost-effective.* Most common selection models are not expensive. In fact, the nonnumeric models themselves do not cost anything. However, they can be expensive in terms of labor hours needed to emply them or program them for general use. Numeric models, particularly highly sophisticated simulations, can require initial capital outlay for the software or for the cost of the labor to program them. Regardless, the model should never be more expensive than the projects they are analyzing. They should be as economical as possible and still be as sophisticated as needed to do the required analysis.

Nonnumeric Selection Models

Q-Sort Model

An excellent method for prioritizing projects within an organization is called the Q-Sort method.[2] This method is by far one of the most straightforward nonnumeric methods and can be used for anything that involves prioritization of events or projects or for identification of problems.

In general, the Q-Sort method follows this initial procedure:

1. Write the potential projects on 5 × 7–inch index cards, one project per card.
2. Divide the stack of cards into three stacks: good, fair, and poor. Good, fair, and poor are subjective measures of the relative worth to the organization of the projects being considered. So it is important that participants be knowledgeable about the company's business so that project merits can be assessed and ranked. The number of cards per stack does not have to be equal, but none of the stacks should have more than eight cards.
3. If any of the stacks has more than eight cards, the cards are further divided into better and worse groups. For example, if the "poor" stack has more than eight cards, it can be subdivided into better-than-average poor, poor, and worse-than average poor.
4. Continue this process until none of the stacks contains more than eight cards.

Once this initial sorting is completed, each of the stacks is then subjected to the Q-Sort process. The Q-Sort process can be done by one person who has the responsibility for the prioritization, but it is better if done by a committee. If the process is done by a committee, each member is given a copy of a stack of cards. Then each participant begins the Q-Sort process, which consists of five steps.

1. Each participant receives a stack of cards containing the project name and any required descriptive information.
2. Each participant divides her stack into two stacks: one being high-priority level and the other being low-priority level. The delineation between high and low levels can be determined by some sort of weighting and measuring criteria or simply based on the participant's best judgment. Remember that these two stacks do not have to be equal in size.
3. Each participant builds a third stack by reexamining both

the high- and low-priority stacks for borderline or ques-
tionable entries. This third stack of cards will become the
medium-priority level.

4. Each participant examines both the high- and low-priority stacks to form two additional stacks of very-high-pri-
ority and very-low-priority stacks. At this point, each
participant should have five stacks representing very
high, high, medium, low, and very low priorities.

5. Each participant may readjust any or all of the stacks as
she sees fit.

A facilitator gathers all the stacks and summarizes and com-
bines them until a consensus is reached. A graphical depiction
of the Q-Sort method is shown in Exhibit 8-1.

Exhibit 8-1. The Q-Sort process.

Source: Adapted from A.F. Helin and W.E. Souder, "Experimental Test of a Q-Sort Procedure for
Prioritizing R&D Projects," *IEEE Transactions on Engineering Management* (November 1974).

Peer Review Method

The peer review method, or a variation of it, is one of the most widely used methods for choosing projects. This is the method most often used by such government agencies as the National Institutes of Health and the National Science Foundation to select projects. It is also often used in other research and development laboratories for prioritizing or selecting projects.

Typically, the peer review method consists of three to five competent people from outside the organization chosen to assess the proposal. Each of these independent evaluators is given a copy of the proposal and asked to rate it against some predetermined criteria. The evaluations are tabulated and compared. Naturally, a project rated low by all or a consensus of the group will not be funded. A project with mixed ratings probably won't be funded either. Only projects receiving high ratings from a strong majority of the group will even be considered.

Closer to home, a variation of the peer review is used in many companies to decide whether to pursue a proposal. This method is especially popular in companies that rely heavily on DOD contracts because it is a fast and easy way to determine whether the company has the technical and resource capability to write a credible proposal and perform the work if it wins the contract. In this version, copies of the solicitation, usually in the form of a Request for Proposal (RFP), are sent to key people who have recognized expertise in the RFP requirements or have experience with the customer and the likely competitors for the business. The facilitator in this process is usually a key marketing or new-business-development person who provides the RFP and whatever additional marketing intelligence is available. Often one or more of the evaluators will express an interest in having the lead for the project should a decision be made to pursue it. Naturally, unless there is strong support or interest in the project, it is not pursued. If there is strong interest in the project, the marketing or new-business-development person and someone from the functional area most likely to be responsible for the contracted work will develop a proposal strategy and a strategy for getting the project on the organization's pursuit list.

Murder Board

The murder board is used in virtually every company in some form for project selection but is especially popular, and useful, in companies dependent on competitive bids for their business. (Its name stems from the fact that members of the board try to find a reason not to pursue a project. In other words, they "kill" it.) The murder board is generally the highest-level board or group that examines potential and ongoing proposal efforts to determine whether a project should be pursued or continued. Furthermore, it is a fast and easy method for selecting and discarding projects.

The senior managers of the organization make up the murder board. Usually that means that each of the vice presidents is automatically a member of the board. The board is usually chaired by the vice president of new business or of marketing, depending on how the organization is structured.

Basically, the murder board meets on a regular basis, usually once a month, to hear briefings on key projects. The key project representative, proposal manager, marketing lead, or project manager, as appropriate, briefs the project to the board. The murder board's function is to disqualify or "kill" the project if it can. That is, the members attempt to find reasons that the organization should not pursue or continue the project. Consequently, the briefer(s) have to be prepared to counter any argument that is made eliminating the project. If they are successful in defending their project to the murder board, then it is allowed to continue to the next phase.

In spite of the ease and usefulness of the murder board, there are three major problems with this approach.

1. It is a negative approach, which impedes brainstorming the potential project for ways to strengthen it and make it viable.

2. It often fosters a competitive environment among the board members to see who can "destroy" the briefer first. The result is that everyone hates going before the murder board and does so reluctantly. The briefings are always designed to short-circuit the board's intent by playing to the biases of the board

members and avoiding any subject that could lead to project disqualification. In short, since the briefer is penalized for identifying potential problem areas, she doesn't. Hence, decisions about the projects are based on incomplete data. If the murder board operates in a collaborative fashion, where risks and concerns are discussed and dealt with, then some projects that might otherwise be disqualified become viable. Furthermore, there would be fewer surprises during the life of those projects that are qualified on inaccurate data.

3. Many people are not good at briefing a hostile audience. As a result, many projects are disqualified because the briefer could not perform well enough, not because the project lacked merit.

Poor Man's Hierarchy

In his book on project management, J. Davidson Frame (a professor of management science at George Washington University in Washington, D.C.) describes a pared-down treatment of a decision-making tool called the analytical hierarchy process (AHP).[3] Frame developed the method as an introduction to the AHP, but the method is a good decision-making tool in its own right. He calls this tool the *poor man's hierarchy*.

The method is straightforward and easy to use. It requires only that some baseline criteria be established against which the project will be measured. A square grid is constructed, and the criteria are listed along the left-hand side and across the top of the grid. Then each individual criterion on the left-hand side of the grid is assessed in turn against all of the remaining criteria across the top of the grid. As each criterion down the left side is assessed, it is assigned a 1 if it is more important than the criteron across the top and a 0 if it is less important. Naturally, the criteria are not assessed against themselves in the process, so the diagonal of the grid is left blank. When all the criteria are assessed in this fashion, the numbers are totaled for each. The criteria are sorted by total rating, largest number first, to rank-order them. This method can be used to assess the criteria of an individual project, as in Exhibit 8-2, or it can be used to prioritize projects within the organization.

Numeric Selection Models

Several numeric selection tools based on complex mathematical models are available. These methods are most often used in a research and development environment where significant risk and uncertainty exist. Since this book is more general in nature, I discuss only the more common selection models here.[4]

Exhibit 8-2. Example of poor man's hierarchy.

	Ada Programming	Cost	Portability	Maintainability	Reliability	Ease of Revision	Total Rating
Ada Programming		1	0	0	0	1	2
Cost	0		1	0	0	0	1
Portability	1	0		0	0	1	2
Maintainability	1	1	1		1	1	5
Reliability	1	1	1	0		1	4
Ease of Revision	0	1	0	0	0		1

Payback Period

One of the most common selection tools is the *payback period*, defined as that period in a project's life cycle after which the cumulative annual cash inflow exceeds the expenditures for the project. The *payback point* is that point where the cumulative revenues exactly equal the expenditures. Usually the expenditures are taken to be the initial investment.

Suppose an organization plans to install a new piece of equipment to make computer chips. The cost of the equipment is $200,000 and the expected annual revenue is $50,000. The payback period is calculated as follows:

$$\text{Payback period} = \frac{200,000}{50,000}$$
$$= 4 \text{ years}$$

Although this method is used often by senior managers and financial officers, it is a poor selection tool because it does not take into account the cost of money, that is, inflation; it assumes that revenues will continue beyond the payback period; and it does not account for risk. An early payback period implies that the risk is less than a later payback period. The fact is that risk is not explicitly considered at all unless a risk factor is included in the calculation of the annual revenues, and that is seldom done.

Average Rate of Return or Return on Investment

The average rate of return (ARR) is another favorite selection tool, but it suffers from the same disadvantages that the payback method does: It does not account for the cost of money, does not consider future profits, and assumes there is less risk the larger the rate of return.

The primary reason for discussing the ARR method here is to point out a common mistake: Most people assume the ARR is just the inverse of the payback period. Notice, though, that the payback period definition includes annual revenues. The definition of ARR is the cost of initial investment divided by the annual expected profits.

Suppose in the example of the payback period that the expected annual profits are $20,000. Then the average rate of return is:

$$ARR = \frac{20,000}{200,000}$$

$$= .10 \text{ or } 10\%$$

If we use the inverse of the payback period as the ARR, then the ARR would have been:

$$ARR = \frac{50,000}{200,000}$$

$$= .25 \text{ or } 25\%$$

Considering the shortcomings of this method relative to risks, it is easy to see how false expectations can be generated with the erroneous expectation of a 25 percent rate of return. The problem, of course, is that revenues include profit but other cash inflows as well, such as payment for work completed on a contract.

Neither the payback period nor the ARR method is recommended as a selection tool for the reasons stated. However, both are often used for this purpose principally because they are simple and fast. One advantage of these methods, other than their simplicity, is that they can be used to help plan organizational cash flow. They could also be used as a quick, approximate measure of merit or for measuring the relative rankings of several projects. Otherwise they should be applied with great caution, and never as the only measure, if they are to be used as tools for project selection.

Benefit-to-Cost Ratio

Among the several variations of benefit-to-cost ratio methods, the most widely used one involves calculating the net present value (NPV) of costs and revenues. The NPV predicts the value of today's dollars in terms of its future worth. In other words, it explicitly includes inflation as well as expected or desired profits.

Determining an accurate benefit-to-cost ratio can be very difficult since such things as cost avoidance of labor, maintenance, and efficiency of new equipment or processes have to be quantified. Once that is done, the NPV method yields accurate estimates on which a reasoned decision can be made.

The formula for NPV is:

$$NPV = \sum_{t=0}^{n} \frac{F_t}{(1+k)^t}$$

where:

F_t = future cash flow at time t.

k = rate of return, which can have two components: estimated rate of inflation, i, and required or desired profit, p. Hence, $k = i + p$.

Σ = the mathematical symbol meaning to sum the cash flow for any entry in the range of $t = 0$ through the last period, n.

As an example of the NPV method, suppose we have determined that a new management information system for the organization will require a $50,000 capital expense immediately and another $10,000 in six months. The benefit to the organization will be worth $10,000 at the six-month mark and $20,000 at six-month intervals until the end of the second year. The inflation rate is estimated to be 6 percent, and senior management would like to realize a 12 percent return or profit as a result of the new system. What is the benefit-to-cost ratio for this project?

A sketch of the project costs and revenues is shown in Exhibit 8-3. It is recommended that any analysis using NPV be laid out in this fashion because it helps to keep the time intervals and cash flow categories straight. You will see from the problem that determining the proper value of k is crucial since the magnitude of this term dramatically affects the outcome of the benefit-to-cost ratio analysis.

The NPV for the revenues (NPV_r) is:

$$NPV_r = \frac{10,000}{(1 + .09)^1} + \frac{20,000}{(1 + .09)^2} + \frac{20,000}{(1 + .09)^3} + \frac{20,000}{(1 + .09)^4}$$

Exhibit 8-3. Layout of cash flow estimates.

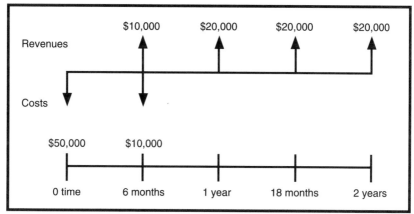

Note that $k = i + p = .06 + .12 = .18$, but the time increments are six-month intervals. Therefore, the rate of return for each six months is .09.

When we perform the operations of the equation above, NPV_r becomes:

$$NPV_r = \frac{10,000}{1.09} + \frac{20,000}{1.19} + \frac{20,000}{1.30} + \frac{20,000}{1.41}$$

$$= 9,174.31 + 16,806.72 + 15,384.62 + 14,184.40$$

$$= 55,550.05$$

We now have to calculate the NPV for the costs of the project (NPV_c):

$$NPV_c = \frac{50,000}{(1 + .09)^0} + \frac{10,000}{(1 + .09)^1}$$

$$= \frac{50,000}{1} + \frac{10,000}{1.09}$$

$$= 50,000 + 9174.31$$

$$= 59,174.31$$

Note that in the first term in the first part of the equation, since the $50,000 costs was required immediately, then $t = 0$ and anything raised to the zero power equals 1. Hence, as you would expect, the $50,000 is not discounted since it is already in current dollars.

To calculate the benefit-to-cost ratio, we simply divide the NPV of the revenues by the NPV of the costs. Hence, for the example, the benefit-to-cost ratio (BCR) is:

$$BCR = \frac{NPV_r}{NPV_c}$$

$$= \frac{55,550.05}{59,174.31}$$

$$= .94$$

To realize a positive return on investment, the BCR has to be greater than one; to break even, BCR has to be one; less than one indicates that costs outweigh the revenues.

The benefits of the example appear to outweigh the costs of the management information system at first glance, but when the future value of the cash flow is accounted for, the benefit-to-cost ratio for the first two years at least clearly shows that the organization cannot expect any positive return on the investment. However, if the benefits from the system continue beyond the second year, it is obvious that the payback period would occur shortly after the second year and the BCR will be greater than one. If the benefits are not expected to continue after the second year, then management would have to lower its expectations about the desired rate of profit as a result of the new system.

Selecting a Project Manager

Once the project is selected, the real problem is choosing the right project manager to run it. The project manager is the key to a successful project. Choosing the wrong person can quickly turn what could have been a profitable endeavor into an economic and political disaster.

Only fifteen to twenty years ago, project managers were

chosen from those who had the most seniority or had been successful project engineers. It was almost universally accepted that project managers had to be engineers. It was rare that a project manager had had any formal project management training; all project management was done on the job. This type of experience and training is not all bad; working on a project is the best classroom there is. But it has now been recognized that there is more to running a project successfully than just understanding how to schedule work or prepare progress reports. The project manager needs a whole host of skills as was treated in the discussion of project management skills in Chapter 1.

Organizations are being more selective about whom they choose to put in the project management pool, and they are beginning to ensure that these people have the requisite skills, training, and experience. Just as being the top salesperson does not ensure that the person will be a good director of marketing, neither does being a good project engineer ensure that the person will succeed as a project manager. The basic skills needed by a successful project manager fall into four categories: personal characteristics, behavioral skills, general business skills, and technical skills.

Personal Characteristics

The most important personal characteristics needed by a successful project manager are:

- Flexible and adaptable
- Possessing and exhibiting initiative and leadership
- Confident and persuasive
- Possessing verbal fluency
- Able to balance technical and human components of a project
- Problem-solving and decision-making capability
- Good time manager

See Archibald Russell's book for a much expanded discussion on this subject.[5]

I would add one more: a sense of humor. Given that the work life of a project manager is a life of conflict, a sense of humor is absolutely critical for one's own well-being.

Behavioral Skills

Gone are the days when project managers could successfully complete a project through intimidation and a heavy-handed management style. The real key to success is through leadership, mentoring, coaching, and negotiation. The project manager must have a strong, active, and continuing interest in teaching, training, and developing subordinates. Without these skills, the project manager may succeed in the short term, but the long-term damage is irreparable. Strong interpersonal skills and the ability to listen actively and communicate are requirements if the project manager hopes to get unqualified support from the project team, the customer, and the rest of the organization.

General Business Skills

A project, large or small, is like a little company in which the project manager is the general manager. A general business education, formal or not, is crucial to guiding the project through its life cycle in consonance with the strategic goals of the parent organization. Most project managers are given the profit-and-loss responsibility of the project and of necessity have to understand what that means and how to manage within the bounds of solid business practices. The project manager's business skills include the following:

- Understanding the organization and the organization's core business
- Understanding marketing, control, contracting, purchasing, law, personnel administration, and the general concept of profitability
- Understanding the concept of direct and indirect cost allocation
- Understanding how to translate business requirements into project and system requirements

Technical Skills

There is no question that the successful project manager must possess some technical competence in the technical area of the project. The premise that the project manager is technically knowledgeable about the project is important if for no other reason than that he won't have any credibility with the other team members if he lacks this knowledge. It is also important that the project manager have some previous management experience within the field, as an assistant project manager, project engineer, or functional manager. However, it is not required that the project manager be an expert in the area of the project. In fact, it is better that the project manager not be an expert in the area of the project because "experts" tend not to be open to suggestions or alternative approaches from the rest of the team members. The recommendation is that the project manager be knowledgeable in the field but be a generalist with a broad knowledge of supporting technology, human relations, management, and communication skills.

The senior management of an organization has the responsibility for hiring and training a cadre of project managers. Choosing the right project manager is not easy because the skill requirements are so broad. The best companies are the ones that successfully accomplish this task.

Summary

Project selection has become more critical to companies since the early 1990s because of changes in the economy, downsizing for efficiency, and generally increased competition. The need for careful attention to project selection by companies focusing on DOD business is particularly important because of the significant decrease in defense spending.

Several project selection tools, both nonnumeric and numeric types, have been discussed in this chapter. The tools presented are relatively easy to use yet provide accurate data on which sound decisions can be made. The key is to use selection tools that provide the most accurate data possible, not just those that provide quick answers. There is nothing wrong in using payback period or rate of return models to get a sense of the viability of a project or to determine the general cash flow requirements. However, relying on these models alone to select a project can lead to disappointment in a project's performance or, worse, complete failure.

Perhaps more important than selecting the right project is picking the right project manager. Even a "bad" project can realize a certain level of success if it is managed by a skillful and well-qualified project manager. The key to project management selection is finding people who are generalists with broad experience and skills as managers, communicators, mentors, trainers, and coaches.

Notes

1. A. F. Helin and W. E. Souder, "Experimental Test of a Q-Sort Procedure for Prioritizing R&D Projects," *IEEE Transactions on Engineering Management* (November, 1974).
2. See ibid. for a more detailed discussion of this method.
3. J. Davidson Frame, *The New Project Management* (San Francisco: Jossey-Bass, 1994).
4. For information about more sophisticated models, see Jack R. Meredith and Samuel J. Mantel, Jr., *Project Management: A Managerial Approach* (New York: Wiley, 1995) and Harold Kerzner, *Project Management: A Systems Approach to Planning, Scheduling, and Controlling*, 5th ed. (New York: Van Nostrand Reinhold, 1995).
5. Archibald Russell, *Managing High-Technology Programs and Projects* (New York: Wiley-Interscience, 1976).

Chapter 9

The Conceptual Phase: Defining the Project

Man . . . walks up the stairs of his concepts, emerges ahead of his accomplishments.

—John Steinbeck

How well and how thorough the activities of the project's conceptual or defining phase are done will determine how successful the project will be. In this phase, the project manager is selected, the project is defined against the customer's requirements and specifications, a core project team is assembled to help plan the project, and all the various pieces of the project plan are started. Exhibit 9-1 depicts the major tasks and activities of this phase and who is responsible for them.

Starting a project and getting it working smoothly require an extraordinary amount of definition, planning, and attention to detail. It is lack of attention to the small things that eventually sidetracks some projects and leaves the project team wondering what happened. Unfortunately, many of us are so anxious to get moving on a project that we jump right into it without giving adequate attention to the upfront definition and planning tasks. It is the old "ready, fire, aim" problem; we fire before we aim, or in this case, we start work before we do the definition and planning. This chapter stresses the importance of project definition and putting together a core team to lay out the basic elements of the project plan.

Exhibit 9-1. Conceptual phase tasks, activities, and responsible parties.

Tasks	Activities	Responsibility
Initiate project.	Select project manager.	Senior management
Analyze and validate the project requirements, specifications, and opportunities.	Assess project opportunity. Develop project scope statement. Review scope with customer.	Project manager
Assemble core project team.	Review project specifications/requirements to identify key members of project team. Develop benefit-cost analysis. Identify needed resources.	Project manager with functional managers
Develop high-level project plan.	Define project. Develop technical solution. Develop technical alternatives. Develop high-level WBS. Identify functional responsibilities. Identify stakeholders. Develop cost and schedule estimates. Perform initial risk assessment. Start developing supporting plans.	Project manager and core team members
Prepare project charter.	Write project charter. Outline communication requirements. Document project manager's responsibility and authority. Write ececutive summary. Obtain project approval and go-ahead.	Senior management with project manager

Initiating the Project

The Project Manager

Once senior management makes the decision to pursue a project, the first step is to assign a project manager and give him the authority and responsibility to proceed with the activities of the conceptual phase. This moment when the project is handed off is critical for the project manager and for the project. The project manager too often lets the moment pass without obtaining all the information available on the project. Often when a person is informed that he is to assume responsibility for a new project, he walks away too excited, or in some cases too stunned, to think to ask penetrating questions about the project. If the project is a result of a contract from outside the organization, then there will be significant contractual information available already, such as statements of work (SOW) and specifications. But if the project is internal to the organization, there is usually little or no substantive documentation available. The project manager must obtain all the information possible about the project by interviewing the key people who had any part in assessing and selecting the project. Of particular importance is determining who was for and who was against doing the project. (We will discuss the importance of stakeholder support later in this chapter.) The project manager may have to be a pest, but gathering all the basic and defining information at this stage will save a lot of time and headaches later.

The Core Project Team

Any project manager will have a sense of the scope and skills required for the project but usually will not have the expertise to define the project, determine the type and number of people needed for it, write all the supporting plans needed, develop the schedules, and work out the budget by himself. That would not be a wise endeavor even for someone who did have that breadth of expertise; working as a team reduces the risk of missing important elements of a project.

Once the project manager has gathered all the basic data, the next step is to form a team to help define and plan the project. This initial team is called the *core project team* or the *plan development team*. The team comprises experienced people who represent the various functional groups, but they may not be the project team once the project gets underway. At this stage in the project, the project manager's focus is to determine exactly what is to be the final product(s) and how best to accomplish the work. The challenge is to organize a group of subject matter experts who can define the project. The project manager will have to do this with the help and advice of the functional managers. Forming the core team is the first test of the project manager's negotiation and team-building skills.

Analyzing and Validating the Project Opportunity, Requirements, and Specifications

Assessing Project Opportunity

Every project is an opportunity. But how much of an opportunity? If the project results from winning a competitive contract, the bid price to win the contract may be so low that the company can't afford to perform. This dilemma occurs more often than you might think since the overriding criterion in a competitive bid is the price. Similarly, internal projects need to be assessed against company goals and costs to determine whether the benefits outweigh the overall costs.

The major tool for assessing project opportunity is the benefit-to-cost analysis, discussed in the previous chapter. Although this analysis is usually done during the project selection process, a new analysis should be done in the conceptual phase to make certain that all the benefits and all the costs are accounted for. As the requirements and specifications are reviewed or developed, it is not unusual to discover that what appeared to be a promising project may be too costly or too complex for the organization to tackle. Or, on a more optimistic note, it may be that the opportunity is much better than originally thought, and many more opportunities may be spawned from this one. In any event, analyzing the opportunity to determine the impact on the organization is required for planning the cash flow, resources, and technology requirements and to provide a basis for approval for project go-ahead. Remember that there are, or should be, go/no-go decision points at various milestones in the project's life cycle, and the end of the conceptual phase is a major one.

Reviewing the Opportunity Alternatives

Assessing the opportunity has built-in advantages other than just determining if the project is viable. This assessment provides the team a chance to look at and develop other approaches to the technical solution. In the process of analyzing the project requirements, corporate capability, and resources, a better way of attacking the project may emerge.

One of the most beneficial results of the opportunity and opportunity alternatives assessment is that there is of necessity a technology assessment as well. It is through this technology assessment that the project manager can begin to make some trade-offs on the materials needed for the project, make-or-buy decisions, and vendor selections. This is the area where cost reductions can occur and schedule improvements can be made. For example, in the technology assessment, it may be determined that an alternative piece of equipment will work just as well as the originally planned item and will cost less. It also might be found that it is more cost-effective and better for the schedule to subcontract some parts of the work, particularly if the parent organization has limited expertise in one or more areas.

Assessing the opportunity and the opportunity alternatives are not just exercises to make sure all the squares have been checked. Performing these assessments rigorously and in detail will help the project team optimize the technical approach and usually will uncover ways to improve the cost and schedule profiles.

Developing the Project Scope Statement and Project Charter

Perhaps the most difficult part of the project management process is determining what the customer really wants. I often hear project managers complain that their customer cannot define what the product is to be, what its functions are, and what technology to use. Many times the customer does not know either, and it becomes an exercise in frustration for both the customer and the project manager to try to scope the project. This lack of definition can increase the cost of the project and create false starts that affect the schedule.

When I talk about project scope, I mean a description of what the project is supposed to accomplish, how big the product is, how long it will take, what types of skill sets are needed to accomplish the project, and approximately how many resources. In short, scope defines what is to be done, how it is to be done, and how long it will take. Scope definition is determined from and consists of:

- Requirements definition
- WBS development
- Requirements analysis
- Design, development, and implementation concept development
- Completion criteria, that is, quality requirements definition
- Customer acceptance test procedures definition

Reviewing the Opportunity With the Plan Sponsor

The sponsor of a project is the person, functional group, or organization that will finance the project. The sponsor may or may not be the ultimate customer but is the project manager's primary customer at this stage of the project life cycle.

Clearly it is important to include the sponsor or customer, whether external or internal to the organization, in the opportunity assessment process. Participation helps the customer refine her own thinking about what she wants the project to accomplish and helps the project manager develop the project scope. It is far better to help the customer define the project early than to muddle through several iterations to produce something that the customer may eventually decide she likes.

Assembling the Core Project Team

The core project team assembled early in the conceptual phase of the project helps with the planning and scope development; these individuals, however, may or may not be part of the final team. In fact, they usually won't be a member of the project team because the core team often is made up of supervisory-level individuals. They are in positions and possess the expertise to define resource and technical requirements, and therefore to define exactly who should be on the team; however, it is not usually they who actually do the project tasks.

Although the initial team's principal responsibility is to prepare the project plan, not do the actual project work, it is far better that the members of this team be the ones who will eventually be tasked to do the work. After all, they have the best understanding of what is required for each task in terms of resources, costs, and schedules. Besides, using the project team members at this stage will foster a better understanding of the requirements, and it will be an excellent way to begin building team spirit and commitment. Therefore, it is crucial to identify project team members as early as possible and to identify those who will remain team members until their expertise is no longer required. Frequent team changes tend to reduce morale and project commitment.

Obtaining Commitments

Once the required resources are identified, the real challenge of getting functional management commitment begins. Negotiating for resources is a constant task of the project manager. That is why negotiating skills rank high on the list of required skills for the successful project manager. (Refer to Chapter 5 for guidance in negotiating with the functional managers.)

The best approach to obtaining the functional manager support is by showing them how the project will benefit their group. This approach requires the project manager to be prepared to discuss the project in depth. One of the most useful tools for this purpose is a talking paper or short paper that succinctly describes the project. (A talking paper is a one- or two-page paper in a bullet or list format summarizing the subject. It is used in much the same way a speaker uses index cards, hence the name.) I often leave this paper with the functional managers so that they can read it over at their leisure. It is important, though, to have orally described the project in enough detail that it will be easy for the functional manager to agree with the project manager's request.

Knowing Who You Want and Asking for Them

Too many project managers approach the functional groups with a request for resources without identifying specific individuals—a serious mistake, because the tendency is to supply people who are not strong project team members or who have less experience and skill. In other words, the functional manager would much prefer to keep her best staff available for the functional requirements of the group.

The project manager should always approach this task with specific names of the subject matter experts needed. It won't be possible for the functional managers to accommodate the project manager every time because the requested individuals may be committed to other projects already. Nevertheless, by naming specific individuals, the project manager defines the skill level desired from the functional group. The project manager can then take the position that if the requested individuals are not available, then someone of the functional manager's choice will suffice as long as the person possesses the same, or better, qualifications. To begin negotiations for less qualified people will guarantee less qualified people.

Assigning Resources to Planning

As each member of the team is identified, he or she should be assigned to developing the project charter and project plan. The project manager's responsibility at this stage is to provide an abbreviated orientation for the project team, make specific assignments for analyzing the requirements and specifications, and begin writing the plans.

There is a lot of pressure on the project manager to get the project rolling. The customer wants to see progress as soon as possible, and the senior managers tend to be impatient for action too. Progress is not progress unless it is visible. Perhaps that is why so many projects get started with inadequate planning. There is no question that it is imperative to have a kick-off meeting and to get the project moving as quickly as possible, but it is more important to define the project completely and produce a plan that will guide the team to a successful conclusion to the project. It will test the project manager's mettle, but firm resistance, within the realm of good judgment, to the pressure of kicking off the project too soon will pay dividends in the long run.

Developing a High-Level Project Plan

This early in the project, it is difficult to have enough information to write a detailed plan. The objective at this stage is to write a high-level plan that can be used to develop a project charter and to ensure that the customer and the parent organization agree with the requirement definition and the proposed technical approach. That is not to say that a great deal of work isn't required; in fact, this part of the project cycle is laying the groundwork for the planning process in the next phase of the project's life cycle.

Stakeholder Analysis

A stakeholder is anyone or any organization that is involved in or may be affected by project activities. In my seminars, I am constantly struck by how many project managers remark, after a discussion about stakeholders, that they could now understand why their project was not completely successful: They had failed to identify the stakeholders and to keep them properly informed about the project.

The project manager and the core team need to identify all the stakeholders as soon as possible. Exhibit 9-2 is a simple form to use in stakeholder analysis. The form has provisions for indicating whether the stakeholder is for or against the project or is neutral. A stakeholder who has negative feelings about a project or is neutral. A stakeholder who has negative feelings about a project can scuttle it before the project manager knows what happens. It is absolutely critical to identify all the stakeholders and determine who has negative feelings and why. The form also has a place to record strategies for winning over negative and neutral stakeholders. The idea is twofold: to win over the negative stakeholders so that the project efforts won't be sabotaged and to change the negative and neutral stakeholders into allies.

Most of the time, it is easy to identify stakeholders: the functional manager who supplies the personnel for the project, the customer, and the project manager's direct superior, for example. The difficulty comes when trying to identify individuals or groups who have indirect or downstream involvement with the project—for example, the person or group with the responsibility for maintaining the product after the project to produce it is complete, the conservation group with concerns about how the project's results will affect the environment, and the regulatory agency interested in whether the project meets government standards. The conservation and the regulatory groups don't have direct interests in the project itself, but they do have an interest in how it is administered and what it produces.

Another major purpose of the stakeholder analysis is to determine who needs what kinds of reports. Some stakeholders have no need for and do not care about having status reports more often than, say, quarterly. Some require only high-level overviews of the progress. But others will need to have or will want detailed reports on a frequent basis. The analysis will help the project team to determine what level of detail to provide and how often to provide it.

Exhibit 9-2. Stakeholder analysis form.

Stakeholders	Position			Reason for Position	Strategy to Change Position
	For	Neutral	Against		

Evaluating the Requirements

The project manager's major task during this phase is to evaluate and define the requirements. The sources for determining the requirements include:

- The project contract (if the project results from a competitive bid)
- The statement of work
- Specifications, that is, product requirements, prepared by the customer
- The WBS
- The delivery schedule
- Other documented customer and user inputs

If the project customer is internal to the organization, there will not be a documented specification or SOW. That is why it is very critical for the project manager to determine who in the organization had any part in choosing or creating the project, what the rationale and need are behind the project, and who in the organization supports and does not support the project. In short, the usual onus for developing requirements for an internal project lies more with the project manager and project team than with the customer. Requirements definition is done by answering the questions in Exhibit 9-3, but generally the objective is to determine exactly what is being produced, what its function is, who is going to use it, how it will be integrated into other systems, how long it will take to produce it, and how much it will cost.

When the project team members are satisfied they understand the requirements, the project manager reviews the requirements with the customer to ensure that the team's understanding of what the customer wants agrees with the customer's intent. With customer agreement secured, the project team can now define the project.

Developing the Project Definition

Once the requirements are completely defined and analyzed, defining the project is relatively easy. Developing the project defi-

Exhibit 9-3. Project requirements checklist.

What will the project final product(s) be?
What is the product's function?
How does the product work?
What are the product's physical characteristics?
What are the product's performance characteristics?
How reliable must the product be, and what are the criteria
  for determining reliability?
Does the product have to be integrated into other systems?
If the product is to be integrated into other systems, what are
  the interface requirements?
Who will use the product, and how will it be used?
Does the user have to be trained to operate the product?
Who provides the training for the product? Is training part of this project?
Who will maintain the product after it is placed in service?
What documentation is required for this product?

nition means agreeing on a technical approach to the project, determining what tasks have to be accomplished and how much they will cost and how long they will take, what the likely problems or risk areas are, and what additional plans have to be written.

A Proposed Technical Solution

The initial project team is composed of subject matter experts from the various functional groups of the organization. As the experts, it is they who can best determine the technical solution for the project. The project manager has to guide the process, but it should be a team solution for producing the product.

In many cases, it may be politically wise for the project manager to approach the functional managers for advice and input relative to the technical approach. This approach is particularly helpful if the functional manager does not fully support the project. Most of us are flattered when our advice is sought, and this approach often gains an ally. Also, we often receive solid advice that strengthens the technical approach.

Developing a technical solution should also be a time to

assess the potential risk areas and come up with contingency plans to cope with these problems. It is not possible to determine all the risks ahead of time, but from historical data, it is certainly possible to identify the problems that similar projects had and to plan for them. Many project managers fail to plan for these contingencies and have to deal with them in a reactive manner rather than having work-around plans that allow for a proactive approach to risk.

A High-Level WBS

The WBS is the most important tool of the project manager because all the other tools can be developed from it. At this stage, though, about the best we can do is a high-level WBS— that is, to the second or, better, the third level. It may be possible to develop the WBS to a lower level if the project is similar to previous ones done by the organization. Although there is no WBS that applies to all projects, it is certainly feasible to create a WBS template using applicable boilerplate material. For instance, certain functions, such as the project management function and documentation procedures and publication, are nearly the same for each project. Then the WBS has to be tailored to the individual project. The major objective here is to develop the WBS to a level that will allow the project manager to identify functional responsibilities and a reasonably good estimate of cost and schedule.

Functional Responsibilities

The project manager must always remember that it is the functional groups and the functional managers who are responsible for accomplishing the technical solution to the project. This means that the project manager has the oversight responsibility to see that the project is accomplished in accordance with the customer's requirements, but the functional staff actually do the work. Hence, it is crucial for the project requirements to be defined completely so that each required task is identified. That is the major purpose of the high-level WBS. Once the functional requirements are identified, the project manager can start the negotiating process for these resources.

Cost and Schedule Estimates

The WBS is not a schedule, but all the elements needed to develop the schedule are contained within it. As the WBS is developed, each task and subtask unfold so that the project requirements, functional responsibilities, and individual subject matter expert requirements are identified. Once the WBS is developed to a level low enough to designate it as a work package and identify an individual to do the work, then schedules and budgets can be determined. Also, when the WBS is completely defined, task interdependencies can be determined, and a network analysis can be performed.

High-Level Risk Assessment

There has been a growing awareness of the susceptibility of projects to risk and the need to manage risk consciously. It may seem to be a given that project managers closely monitor and manage risk. The fact is, though, risk is usually considered to be negative, and in the past, the corporate environment of many organizations did not encourage reporting risks or potential risks. Too many senior managers were not open to bad news, and risks were categorized as bad.

In the late 1980s, risk became recognized as something normal in every project, and rather than try to hide the potential for it, risk is now identified and managed. Furthermore, risk is no longer viewed as a pure loss situation; it is viewed equally as an opportunity. *Risk management* is a process of identifying the risk, determining whether there is opportunity or loss potential with it, and planning ways to handle it. The identification of risk has to start in the conceptual phase in order to define the technical solution, determine make-or-buy strategies, and make plans insomuch as is possible to deal with the risk.

Naturally, all risks cannot be identified at this stage of the project. The project manager and the initial team have to rely on experience and historical data to identify potential risks. Exhibit 9-4 shows a simple form for risk identification. The form is divided into the three broad categories of budget, schedule, and performance or quality since these are the three major elements of the project that the project manager is concerned with. These categories can be further divided into specialized categories to fit the individual project. Bear in mind that at this stage, we are concerned with a very high-level risk assessment for planning purposes, but risk will be considered in greater detail in the planning phase and will receive attention throughout the project life cycle.

Supporting Project Plans

The final step in the initial project planning stage is to develop supporting plans that serve to keep the project running smoothly, inform stakeholders and project team members of progress, and provide a baseline for meeting the technical speci-

Exhibit 9-4. Risk assessment form.

Risk Area	Potential Problem	When and How It Could Occur	Alternative Action
Budget			
Schedule			
Quality			

fications. Supporting plans range from fairly simple and straightforward matrices that show who receives progress or status reports and the level of information to be portrayed, to very detailed and complex documents that show the level of reliability of a product and how to measure it. Generally each project will have a technical plan showing the general approach, a communication plan showing who will receive what type of status reports and how often, a project review plan, a technical performance measurement plan(s), and resource allocation plans. These plans will be part of the overall project management plan and will either be embedded in the master plan or, if fairly large and complex, will be attached as appendixes. A rule of thumb about planning and the depth of plans is to plan to a level of detail that is commensurate with the amount of monitoring and control needed. Extremely careful monitoring and control requirements need very detailed plans; for periodic monitoring and relatively little control from the project manager, high-level planning will suffice.

Preparing the Project Charter

The culmination of the conceptual phase is to prepare a *project charter*, a document, prepared by senior management in conjunction with the project manager, that briefly outlines the project scope, names the project manager, identifies the required resources, and establishes the communication plan for the project. The charter is the primary vehicle for identifying the parameters of the project and can be a powerful communication and negotiation tool. It is the vehicle for obtaining buy-in from the functional managers and for obtaining final approval to continue with the project. Exhibit 9-5 provides a general outline for a charter.

As important and useful as charters are, very few organizations require or use them. Perhaps it is because there is a lack of understanding about project management and project management procedures, or perhaps many organizations view the project management plan as the charter. Whatever the reason, it is

Exhibit 9-5. Project charter outline.

I.	Purpose
II.	Project Establishment
III.	Project Manager Designation and Authority
IV.	Project Manager Responsibility
	A. Support organization's responsibilities
	B. Project organization and structure
	C. Project team composition
V.	Project Initiation
	A. Formal project plan
	B. Approved budgets
	C. Approved plan
VI.	Project Personnel
	A. Assignments to projects
	B. Reporting structure
	C. Performance appraisals
VII.	Communication Plan
VIII.	Definitions
IX.	Appendixes

in the project manager's best interest to push for a project charter because it establishes her authority and provides the parameters for the project, including an estimate of resources. The project charter provides the project manager with additional leverage when negotiating with the functional managers because in all likelihood, they will have been part of the charter preparation and will already have agreed, or, at the minimum, be on notice that they have an obligation, to support the project.

A charter is not required if the project results from a contract outside the organization because the contractual documents, along with the original proposal, serve as the charter. Otherwise, the project manager should always push to have a charter developed. Remember that the project manager and the initial project team will provide much of the input that makes up the charter, but senior management is responsible for preparing the final document.

After the project charter is completed and final approval to go ahead with the project is obtained, the project manager is ready to assemble the full project team and kick off the project. Their first priority is to finalize the project plan, organize the project team, and prepare to implement the project.

Summary

The conceptual phase of the project is the defining phase. During this phase, the project manager puts together a core project team, and together they define the project. The project definition requires a complete understanding of the requirements, the technical skills needed, the personnel and capital resource needs, and who has a vested interested in the project. Attention to detail is probably more critical in this phase than in any other phase of the project.

A project charter is a document prepared by senior management with input from the project manager. This document provides the authority to the project manager to run the project, and it delineates the responsibilities of the various supporting groups of the organization. It also outlines the team members' responsibilities and reporting chain. Many companies don't bother with developing a charter. However, it is in the best interest of the project manager to push for one because it provides a certain amount of leverage when he has to negotiate for resources.

For projects won on a competitive basis—that is, there is a formal contracting document associated with the project—the contract itself serves as the charter. Nevertheless, it is much cleaner and clearer to have a separate document that addresses project policy and philosophy. A charter should be a routine part of the project initiation process. It protects the project manager as well as the organization.

Chapter 10

Project Management in Different Organizational Environments

Management means getting things done through the active support of other people.

—Harold Kerzner, professor of Systems Management,
Baldwin-Wallace College, Berea, Ohio

Virtually every book on project management includes a section on organizational structures, and they all discuss the three most common structures: functional or traditional, project management, and matrix. To be sure, these are the three basic organizational structures on which all other structures are modeled. In my experience, though, two additional organizational concepts deserve attention.

The fact is that few organizations are organized in one of the ideal forms. They are a mixture of two or more of the three basic types or they are a variation of one of them. Also, I have observed that in every single one of my project management classes, there has been at least one student who works in a "non-organizational" organization or a start-up company not yet large enough to need a formal organizational structure.

Why Understanding Organizational Structures Is Important

The project manager has no influence on the way a company is organized. So why is it important to study and understand organizational structures? There are actually several important reasons every project manager has to understand organizational structures:

1. Each structure imposes its own unique advantages and disadvantages relative to the ease of managing a project.

2. The project manager will have greater success working with management, stakeholders, and functional groups if he understands the relationship of each to the project.

3. In those many instances when the project manager has to negotiate for resources, understanding the organizational structure will allow him to maneuver through the intricate maze of responsibility and authority lines.

4. Organizational structures apply to more than the project manager's organization. The project manager is also responsible for working with the customer, vendors, and other company team members. All of these entities have their own unique organizational structures, and understanding the other person's organization will make dealing with them easier.

5. Since today's workforce is so nomadic and most markets are extremely dynamic, it is absolutely certain that every project manager will experience several different organizational structures during his career, even if he stays in the same company.

Types of Organizational Structures

There are three basic types of organizational structure: functional or traditional (hereafter referred to as the functional organization), project management, and matrix. In addition, there are the nonorganizational organizations and the mixture of the basic three types, usually that of functional and matrix organization.

Functional Organization

The functional organization, the oldest of the organizational types, was "invented" by the Roman army and was the structure design model of choice until the mid-1900s. This organization worked well, and still does, as long as the business is not complex or diverse and the company doesn't compete in a dynamic market. Manufacturing and engineering companies often are organized in this fashion.

The functional organization is organized along core competency or functional lines. The structure is well known and follows the general form of the example in Exhibit 10-1.

When a company is organized along functional lines, each project is matched with the functional group that has the greatest interest in seeing it successfully completed. That is, a mechanical engineering project would be placed in the mechanical engineering group, an electrical engineering project in the elec-

Exhibit 10-1. Functional or traditional organization.

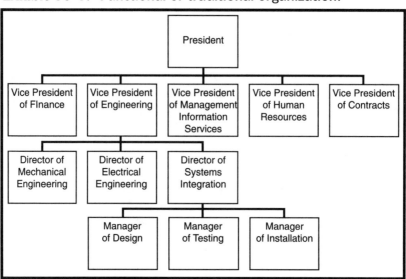

trical engineering group, and so on. There are a number of advantages for project management in this type of organizational hierarchy:

1. Most functional groups contain the requisite technical capability to accomplish the project, and the functional organization accommodates the flexibility required to access this expertise.

2. Individual experts can support a number of different projects of the same class or type.

3. There isn't a loss of technical expertise when a person leaves the company. Because the technical expertise can be grouped and shared within the function, there remains a continuous technical base even as various experts change jobs and move out of the group or company.

4. The functional organization historically has been the path of career advancement for members who have expertise in the functional area. Therefore, team members always have a feeling of home even after the project ends.

As logical and straightforward as this sounds, there is a price to pay for being functionally organized:

1. The customer is not the focus of the project manager's concern. Often the functional arrangement places several levels of management between the project manager and the customer, particularly an external customer. Even when there are not many layers of management between the project manager and the customer, the project manager's primary focus is on the activities and requirements of the functional group rather than on the project requirements.

2. It is not always clear who is in charge of the project. The project manager's functional superior often interjects herself into the project, thus causing confusion within the project team and leaving conflicting directions about the project work.

3. Since the project tends not to be in the mainstream of the functional life, there is usually a lot of difficulty in motivating the project team. Often the team member's performance goals

don't include project work. Hence, there is less interest in achieving the project goals. In fact, the team member may view the project assignment as a secondary duty.

4. If the project is large and complex, requiring expertise from other functional areas, it is difficult to obtain the coordination and teamwork required to accomplish the task expeditiously, and it is virtually impossible to design, build, or manage the project from a holistic perspective.

5. Functional organizations tend to foster internal competition among the functional groups to the extent of creating a nonteam work or noncooperative atmosphere between them.

The Project Organization

From the perspective of the project manager, the project organizational structure is the best possible organization to work in. From the perspective of the corporation, it can be one of the worst.

The pure project organization is one that organizes around each of its projects. That is, each project has assigned to it all the requisite skills, technical and administrative, needed to accomplish the work. Such an organization is depicted in Exhibit 10-2.

The project organization is a good one for the project manager and the project for a number of reasons:

1. There is no doubt who is charge. The project manager has total responsibility for the project and the people and resources assigned to it.

2. The project manager has functional or line responsibility for the people working on the project.

3. The project is customer focused. The project manager can make instantaneous decisions about the project and can react immediately to any customer changes.

4. There is a unity of command. The project team members report to only one boss.

5. If the project elicits a strong identity, the team members usually develop a strong commitment to it and the project manager.

Exhibit 10-2. The project organization.

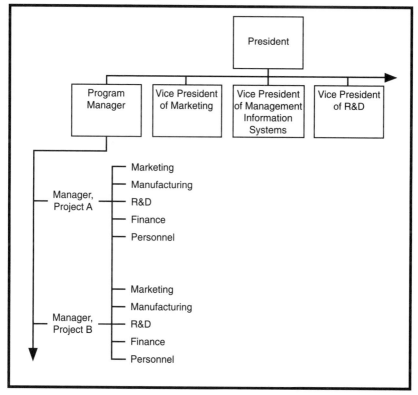

6. The project management organizational structure supports a holistic approach to the project.

As strong is the project organization concept is, there are some equally strong reasons that it does not work for every organization:

1. When the company is project driven and has several active projects at any given time, the duplication of completely staffing each project is a financial drain.

2. Duplicating the support functions (administrative, legal, contractual, human resources, and marketing) drives the over-

head costs so high that the company may become noncompetitive in the market.

3. A project team that is not in the functional mainstream tends to ignore company policies and procedures and can create severe long-term problems with customers. A customer might not like the way it is treated on a succeeding project if it was accustomed to having the previous project team cut corners for it.

4. Project managers tend to keep technical expertise on the payroll after they finish their tasks because they don't want to lose the expertise. And the project manager will hire technical expertise against the time they will be needed just to ensure their availability.

5. If the project is long and has very high visibility, it tends to take on a life of its own. Although that is good for morale and camaraderie, it can be very difficult for the project manager to bring it to closure. The team members don't want the project to end and may sabotage the effort to conclude the project.

Matrix Organization

With the functional and project management structures on the opposite ends of the organizational spectrum, a new concept of organizing for success was needed. The matrix organization is an attempt to mitigate the disadvantages of the functional and project organizations while capitalizing on the advantages of both. The result, an overlay of the project organization onto the functional organization, is shown in Exhibit 10-3. The addition of the program management function places a project advocate in the organizational hierarchy on a par with the other functional leadership.

The numbers against each of the projects in Exhibit 10-3 refer to the amount of time per week (or month) required of a person from each of the functional areas. That is, a marketing person is needed to work on project 1 for $1^1/_2$ days per week. Four days of marketing support are needed for project 2. Note that the same person may support two or more different projects.

Exhibit 10-3. Matrix organization.

	Manufacturing	Marketing	Finance	R&D	Personnel
President					
Program Manager					
PM1	3	1 1/2	1/2	4	1/2
PM2	1	4	1/4	1 1/2	1/4
PM3	0	1/2	3	1/2	1

The advantages of the matrix organization follow:

1. The project is the emphasis, and the customer is the focus.
2. The project team can draw from the functional technical expertise across the organization. This arrangement is even better than in a project organization because of a larger technical base.
3. The project team can draw from the support staff as needed without having to maintain its own. The corporate staff can support many different projects without duplicating staff functions.
4. It is generally easier for the company to balance resources even if there are several simultaneous projects.

The matrix organization has significant advantages over the other two forms; nevertheless, there are still some serious disadvantages:

1. The strength or weakness of the project is a direct function of the strength of the project manager. If she is a strong manager and commands the respect and authority of the functional managers, the project will take on the characteristics of the project management organization. Otherwise, it tends to look like a project in a functional organization. This balance can be very fragile.

2. The matrix concept violates the unity of command, its most serious disadvantage. That is, the team members report to the project manager for project direction and are responsible to her for accomplishing the project's goals, but they still work for a functional manager. Maintaining the proper balance and perspective in this relationship can be very difficult for both the project manager and the team member. The team member's loyalty will always be first with the functional boss, who writes the performance reports.

3. Projects in the matrix concept tend to have serious problems when it becomes time to terminate them. (This is the same problem that occurs in a project organization.) Team members

may block project termination because of the fear that they won't have a functional home to return to once the project ends.

4. Strangely enough, it is not always clear who is in charge in a matrix organization. It happens occasionally that the director or vice president of program management interposes herself into the project. Also, if the project manager isn't careful, the functional managers will assert themselves as the driving force behind the project.

Mixed Organizations

In reality, there are very few pure functional, project, or even matrix organizations. Most organizations are a mixture of two or more of these types. Even when a company strives to organize along the lines of a matrix organization, the strength of the project manager will determine whether the project operates as it would in a functional or project organization. If the pure functional concept is at one end of the organizational spectrum and the pure project concept is at the other, then the pure matrix concept is halfway between the two. But if the project manager is strong in terms of representing her project forcefully when dealing with the functional hierarchy, then the project tends to operate as or take on the appearance of the project organization. And if the project manager tends to be weaker and subjugates herself to the functional manager, then the project takes on the characteristics of the functional organization. These are some of the ways organizations at least appear to be hybrid or mixed organizations.

Other organizations consciously mix types of organizational structures within the overall framework of the company. For instance, a large corporation may be structured along functional lines at the top levels but in a project or matrix or mixture of the two in the various profit centers. This often happens where the corporation has separate subsidiaries within the company's holdings. It almost always happens in entrepreneurial companies when they begin, particularly if they are in a services market or have a diverse customer base. The corporate headquarters will be functionally organized, while the rest of the company is divided into profit centers that essentially operate as little stand-alone companies. These profit centers will take on an organizational structure that meets their immediate customer needs.

Since there are so many variations for organizational structures, one would think that any company could organize to meet its customers' needs while running smoothly and efficiently and providing employees with the kind of atmosphere they need to grow. Yet we hear frustrations and complaints expressed every day from managers and employees alike about the lack of flexibility of their company or the difficult environment they work in. The problem is that changing an organizational structure is not easy. In theory, it is easy, and on paper, it is easy. But the theory or the new organizational lines on paper can't account for the culture of the organization.

On average it takes about five years to make a radical change in a company's organization and to get to the goals that prompted the change. It takes that long to change the company's culture. There has to be a buy-in by all that the new organization is a better way to do business and take care of the employees' needs than the old organization could manage. Engineering such a major cultural change requires extraordinary leadership from the senior management. Unfortunately, many senior managers lack the special training or knowledge about how to accomplish a cultural shift and to mold a new thinking and action process.

What happens all too often when a decision is made to change the organization is that the senior management directs the functional groups to operate in a cooperative and team-spirited way without making any substantive changes in the structure or the way daily tasks are managed. In other words, the idea is to make a functional organization operate like a matrix organization by directing that the functional groups start cooperating cross-functionally or across the company's horizontal lines. This approach to a hybrid organization worsens any existing problems. The project manager will still have to run the project the same as he would in a functional organization.

The Nonorganizational Organization

The classes I teach in project management are geared toward working adults, generally at the midpoint in their careers. Therefore, all of them have experience in the workplace. In every single class, there is at least one, and usually more, who has never worked in anything but a very small company. Invariably, the discussion about organizational structures reveals that some of these people have difficulty relating to anything in the discussion because their company has no formal organization. This nonorganizational concept is not at all uncommon. The typical entrepreneurial start-up company has no formal structure, sometimes for years. These companies tend to operate on the strength of the personality of the owner, and the owner tends to make all of the day-to-day decisions. This pattern will continue until the company grows so big that the owner can't attend to all the daily decisions, the employees become frustrated because they can't get timely decisions needed to do their jobs, and there are difficulties with recruitment, employee benefits, and work space. Finally, it is decided that the company has to have a formal structure. Until that occurs, though, no one worries or even thinks about staff or line functions.

There are some advantages to running a project in a small company that isn't formally organized:

1. The organization is very flexible, and getting to the top management is usually easy.
2. The project tends to be very focused on the customer.
3. Everyone in the organization tends to pitch in wherever they are needed.
4. Morale is usually high because the company operates like one big family.

As nice as working in a small company sounds, there can be some horrendous disadvantages:

1. These companies often don't have sufficient staff to do all that is necessary or, more to the point, all that they have to do to keep the business afloat.

2. Depending on what phase of growth the company is in or its size, the owner may not be as available as the project demands.
3. Because very small companies tend to be cash limited, the best expertise or technology may not be available to the project manager.
4. Almost everyone in the company is overworked.

Summary

The project manager must have a good understanding of organizational types and structures. Each type of organization imposes its own set of advantages and disadvantages on the project and project manager. Understanding these advantages and disadvantages helps the project manager maximize his ability to maneuver through the corporate hierarchy maze to accomplish the goals of the project. Even project managers who work in what I call nonorganizational organizations have to deal with vendors, teammates, or customers who do have formal organizational structures. Understanding the customer's organization can shed light on how long it might take to get approval for changes in the project or who the stakeholders are in the customer hierarchy. The project manager can then plan accordingly. He is now in a position to plan for demands that are placed on the project's schedule, for instance, that are a result of the customer's organizational peculiarities.

Chapter 11
The Development Phase

Make no little plans; they have no magic to stir men's blood.
—Daniel Hudson Burnham (1846–1912),
Chief of Columbian Exposition Construction

The development phase, sometimes called the planning phase, is where the project is refined and all the preparations for implementing, monitoring, and controlling it are completed. It is also during this phase that the project team membership is determined, and negotiations for these individuals are completed.

The importance of planning cannot be overstated. The conceptual phase is crucial in establishing the bounds of the project and determining the details of exactly what is required as an output of the project, but without a plan to achieve these requirements, the conceptual phase is useless. The activities of the development phase operationalize the activities of the conceptual phase. The first step in this process is to finalize, as much as possible, the project team membership.

Establishing the Project Team

During the conceptual phase, one of the first things the project manager does is to form a core project team. This team usually consists of supervisory or senior employees who have broad experience and expertise in the functional areas of the project. They probably will not become part of the operating project team—at least not many of them will—because the project team needs to consist of people who will actually do the work of the project or supervise key portions of the project's work. The project engineer, for example, might be a senior technical person whose responsibilities revolve more around ensuring that the technical specifications of the project are met than in actually performing the work of building the project. But generally the core project team is an initial team that helps define the project and the project team. By the time the project progresses to this phase, the project manager should have determined precisely what types of resources are required—that is, what skill sets are needed and the levels of experience, and the people he would like on the team by name.

Many inexperienced project managers are reluctant to approach functional managers with specific names. They usually request support to perform certain technical functions and then rely on the functional manager to provide the talent they need. The problem with this approach is that the managers are not likely to assign their best staff members to the project unless they have a direct interest in it—that is, they are a major stakeholder. Usually they keep their best staff members available for the functional group requirements, or they assign those who do not happen to have other contracts to work on, in which case they may or may not be the most highly skilled individuals in the group. The point is that project managers need to approach functional managers with specific requests. It may be that the functional manager is unable to accommodate the request because of previous commitments to other projects, but by making specific requests, the project manager has established the level of expertise and experience needed for the project.

Most organizations use some variation of matrix management. Whether the organization takes on the classical matrix structure or is a traditional structure that supports cross-functional teams, the project manager is faced with a dilemma: She does not have functional authority over project personnel and therefore cannot dictate the team membership. The best she can do is to identify who she wants and then negotiate hard to get them.

Negotiating for Team Members

Project managers must have excellent communication skills and, in particular, excellent negotiation skills. Negotiating for resources is usually a continuing process throughout the project's life cycle because of the constant battle with other functional and project priorities. There are things that the project manager can do, though, that will make the chore of negotiating easier and increase the chances of success.

The best preparation for negotiating for resources is to know the project thoroughly. The project manager should know more about the project—its scope, any contract requirements, technical and personnel requirements, and the final output— than anyone else. Yet many project managers fail in their negotiation attempts because they don't take the next step of organizing and summarizing all their information so that it is succinct, concise, and easily retrievable. The key to negotiating with a functional manager is being able to talk about the project in a way that clearly:

- Explains the goals and objectives of the project.
- Ties the project goals and objectives to the goals and objectives of the organization.
- Shows how the project will directly benefit the functional group.
- Shows why the project requires very specific skill levels and experience.

These four things can be accomplished only if the project manager is thoroughly familiar with every aspect of the project and has consciously thought through each need and step in the project life cycle.

The best approach to preparing for negotiations with functional managers is to write a point paper: a short, succinct paper with bulleted points summarizing the project. Actually, this point paper serves two purposes: It is an excellent way to learn all the aspects of the project, and it is a good document to negotiate from with the functional manager. It is usually a good idea to have something in hand to leave with the functional manager as well, and the point paper serves this purpose nicely.

Assigning Project Staff

As the project team takes shape, each member should be assigned to refining the project and specifically to writing the project plan. As we shall see later in this chapter, the completed project plan requires some detailed analyses leading to the development and use of many of the technical tools discussed in Part One. Hence, the project manager needs to staff the project team with skilled and experienced personnel as quickly as possible. Bear in mind that the project manager's role is not to develop the plan unilaterally but rather to direct the efforts of the team to do it. Most of the project work, especially in the conceptual and planning phases, is best done by a team and as a result of brainstorming each of the issues.

The ideal project team will be one in which the members are the subject matter experts for the project tasks, have significant experience in analyzing and planning project work, are better-than-average writers, and will be the individuals who will actually do the work once the project is implemented.

Project Kickoff

Every project needs a *kickoff meeting,* the first formal meeting of the project team and stakeholders. Where exactly in the process it should occur is a matter of judgment by the project manager. However, the kickoff meeting should be as early in the process as possible. My preference is to have the meeting near the end of, or as the last activity of, the conceptual phase. Sometimes, though, the kickoff meeting best fits somewhere near the beginning of the development phase because of a lack of enough information to conduct a meaningful kickoff meeting. There are those who argue that a kickoff meeting should not be held until the end of the development phase because not enough is known about the project until all the planning has been completed. The problem with this approach is that too much time elapses and the real benefits of the kickoff meeting can't be realized. Holding a kickoff meeting too soon leaves the participants with the feeling that the project is unorganized or lacking in definition. Determining the best time to kick off the project requires a close look at what the meeting is to accomplish.

The kickoff meeting should be scheduled and chaired by the project manager. A word of caution is important. The kickoff meeting is often viewed as being within the purview of the senior manager of new-business development. It is very difficult for the project manager to control the meeting when a senior person feels or thinks she is in charge of it. Therefore, it is very important to establish beforehand whether this type of situation will exist and to try to reach an understanding about what each person's role will be.

Once the roles are established, the kickoff meeting should be scheduled, and all team members and stakeholders should be invited. At this meeting, it is much better to err on the side of inviting too many people than to slight a stakeholder. At a minimum, the kickoff meeting should accomplish the following:

- Introduce the team members and the stakeholders.
- Review the project scope.
- Review the project output—that is, the project's purpose.
- Identify potential risks and preliminary plans to mitigate the risks (it is always wise to discuss known risks at the kickoff meeting because it provides a forum to discuss the risks and often results in plans or strategies that will eliminate the risks altogether).
- Present immediate plans for the project, and describe what each project team member will be doing in the next several days.

It is not difficult to see why many project managers are reluctant to schedule a kickoff meeting until they have completed all the planning. The risk of holding the meeting too soon is that questions may be raised that cannot be answered, resulting in embarrassment for the project manager. Unfortunately, senior management and customers view the kickoff meeting as evidence that the project is moving, and they will want that to occur at the earliest possible time. It is a delicate balance and one that requires judgment and experience from the project manager.

Analyzing the Project Requirements: Preparing to Write the Project Plan

Distinguishing between the conceptual and development phases of the life cycle is difficult because the activities of each are virtually the same. The major difference in the two phases is one of degree of detail. In the conceptual phase, the project manager is concerned with a broad view of the project, that is, the big picture. In the development phase, the project manager is concerned with defining the specific and discrete elements of the big picture.

There are several tasks associated with analyzing and refining the project requirements:

- Understanding customer requirements
- Defining the project objectives
- Defining critical success factors
- Making make-or-buy decisions

Understanding Customer Requirements

If the project manager has diligently evaluated the project requirements during the first phase and verified the evaluation results with the customer, then this step is relatively straightforward. It is simply an opportunity for the project manager to double-check previous assumptions and conclusions about the project and fill in any missing details.

Revisiting the customer requirements at this point is necessary also because the project team is now in place. Therefore, this becomes an opportunity for the project manager to ensure that all the project team members have a complete understanding of the project requirements. Reviewing the requirements with the team at this point has the added advantage that the new team members will have a fresh perspective of the project and its requirements. Hence, there will probably be different, and maybe better, interpretations of the customer's needs that will have to be clarified with the customer.

Defining the Project Objectives

The project objectives—what the project is to accomplish or its reason for being—have to be completely defined. The objectives in large measure define the technical approach. Unless the objectives are clearly understood, the technical solution will either provide a product that can't meet the requirements or one whose capability far exceeds the customer's needs (termed *gold-plating*).

A classic example of the case of exceeding the customer's needs occurred with regularity during the mid-1970s when the DOD, in response to the fuel crisis, started procuring advanced flight simulators to reduce the amount of actual aircraft flight time needed for training. Those of us who were responsible for writing the specifications for this training equipment felt that the simulators had to duplicate real-world conditions as closely as possible. In our defense, we really didn't know any better at the time because no real data existed to the contrary. Consequently, the specifications we wrote were very detailed and required engineering tolerances equally as stringent as on the aircraft being simulated. In fact, we often lifted whole sections of aircraft specifications and used them verbatim in the simulator specifications. In addition, the visual systems we required were good enough to show discrete branches and leaves on trees, as well as moving vehicles on the ground. These stringent specifications drove the cost of our simulators to the point that a single weapons systems trainer—a six degree-of-freedom simulator with air-to-air or air-to-ground fighting capability—cost more than the real aircraft. To make matters worse, no one did an analysis before procuring the training equipment to determine what capability was needed in the simulator or how it could be used most efficiently. Instead, it was built with little or no consultation with the user, and then it was left to the user to structure a training program around the equipment. In other words, the training equipment, not the training, was the focus. Happily, the DOD has realized that the training program itself is where the focus belongs, and simulators, along with whiteboards, overhead projectors, and flip charts, are just training media.

Accurately defining project objectives prior to project implementation, then, is very important.

Defining Critical Success Factors

The project team has to define the factors related to the project that will directly influence whether the project is a success. There are factors—either events happening at particular times or people who have strong interests in the project—that influence whether the project's goals and objectives are met. This is different from the risk assessment, although a critical success factor could also be a risk area. For instance, a critical success factor might be the public support of the project by a senior manager in the organization. However, she may be withholding her support until she sees positive results from an upcoming test. On the one hand, it is critical to the success of the project to have this particular manager's support, but there is a risk that she might not give it.

Other critical success factors could be such things as these:

- Improvements to the components being procured for the project
- Availability of personnel with particular skills
- Strong first article tests results
- Error-free demonstration of the prototype
- On-time and on-budget delivery

Some of these factors may be risks as well, but some of them, such as the error-free demonstration, might provide a tremendous boast to the project if it occurs, but might not be more than a temporary disappointment if it does not occur. Defining these critical success factors early helps the team write them into the project plan so that they can work toward making the success factors a reality.

Making Make-or-Buy Decisions

Once the potential problems and the critical success factors are defined, the team is in a position to assess what has to be done against the organization's capability to do it. Often, it becomes clear that some requirements of the project demand an expertise that does not exist in the organization. To cope with this eventuality, the project manager has essentially three choices:

1. Procure the needed capability from a consultant or from a vendor.
2. Team with one or more organizations that do have the capability.
3. Hire additional personnel who have the required capability.

Generally the third option is not an option at all for the project manager, although there are circumstances in which the project manager might make such a recommendation and the senior management would agree because that provides a capability that could be used for other projects as well. The most likely scenario would be the first or the second choice—hence, the term "make or buy." The project manager, along with the project team, has to make the decision about what part or parts of the project the organization will do and what part or parts of the project it will procure from someone else. Notice that it is not a question of whether the organization can do a particular piece of work, but whether the organization will or should do the work. There may be a perfectly good reason that it would be better to procure a piece of work that the organization has in-depth experience and expertise in. The most obvious reason it might be better to procure some of the work from outside the organization is that a smaller company might be able to do the work at lower cost.

Make-or-buy decisions have tremendous ramifications for a company. Many senior managers will not easily agree to buy a service if the home organization can do it because it means that there will be less coverage, that is, direct charges to the contract, for the manager's employees. Furthermore, organizations cannot allow a teammate to have such a large percentage of the contract that the teammate becomes the prime contractor. But all that notwithstanding, the project manager, theoretically at least, can make the decision to "buy" none, some, or even all of the services and products from outside the organization. Determining what percentage the organization will make and what percentage it will buy is a crucial decision to the planning process.

Writing the Project Plan

The project plan really was begun during the conceptual phase of the project when the scope was defined and high-level budgets, schedules, and resource requirements were estimated. As soon as the project team is established, all the elements of the project plan can be defined and refined, and the plan can be written.

There are five steps in the project planning phase of the project life cycle. Exhibit 11-1 lists these steps and shows the

Exhibit 11-1. Project planning steps and planning tools.

Planning Steps	Project Management Tools
Decompose project into tasks and subtasks.	Work breakdown structure
Determine task durations and interdependencies.	PERT or precedence diagramming charts
Develop project schedules.	Work breakdown structure Gantt Chart
Estimate task costs and develop the project budget.	Work breakdown structure
Determine final resource requirements.	Work breakdown structure Task responsibility matrix

technical tools that the project team can use to accomplish each of the steps.

Decomposing the Project Into Tasks and Subtasks

Decomposing the project into tasks and subtasks is best done through the development of the WBS. The best way to develop a WBS is through brainstorming sessions with the project team, writing each task or subtask on a sticky note and sticking the notes on a wall or whiteboard. Brainstorming reduces the risk of forgetting a task, and sticking the notes on a wall allows the team to consolidate tasks, eliminate duplication, and move the tasks around until the team is satisfied with their placement within the WBS hierarchy.

Once the WBS is developed, any of several project management software packages can be used to put the WBS into its final form. Some of the most popular software packages are Microsoft Project, TimeLine, Primavera, Project Scheduler 6 (PS 6), and SureTrak. All of these software packages will display and print the WBS in the indented format, although not all will display and print it in the graphical format. Microsoft Project is one that does not have the graphical format capabilitiy; PS 6 is one that does.

Determining Task Durations and Interdependencies

Once the WBS is developed, all the other planning tools can be developed too. The next one needed is the precedence diagram (PD) (or PERT as appropriate). (Refer to Chapter 6 for a review of this important tool.) The PD is used to show the interdependencies of the tasks and subtasks. It is necessary to construct the PD because it is only after the network is analyzed that the next step, developing the schedule, can be accomplished. The network logic shows how the tasks relate to each other and which ones can be done in parallel. The network also defines the over-all schedule length.

The PD is developed by first determining how long each individual task and subtask takes. The project manager, or the designated lead person for a specific project area, determines how long the tasks and subtasks take by talking with the individuals who will be doing the work. During the process of determining how long the task takes, the project team should also determine how the task relates to other tasks.

Generally the responsible individual will be able to estimate with great accuracy how long the work will take because that person will have performed the same or similar tasks many times before. This individual will also know what information is required from other tasks before the task can start. Occasionally, the work will be completely new, or the task will involve significant research and development so that estimating the time accuracy is very difficult. In those cases, the project manager, along with the appropriate subject matter experts, will use the PERT analysis technique to determine the schedule.

Constructing the PD network also serves other purposes, but because of the importance of the network analysis and the critical information derived from the analysis, particularly for planning, it is worth repeating what kinds of information can be derived from the analysis:

- Schedule length
- Critical path (the longest path in the network and the path that has zero slack in its activities)
- Total slack in the project and slack by individual task
- A graphical view of how each task relates to every other task

With the network analysis complete, the project team can develop the project schedules.

Developing Project Schedules

An excellent tool for developing and portraying schedules is the Gantt chart, developed around 1917 by Henry Gantt, a pioneer in scientific management. The Gantt chart is, in its basic form, a schedule chart depicting the project tasks and their associated beginning and ending dates. Usually, these dates are connected by a solid bar to graphically portray the task's duration. Exhibit 11-2 is an example of a Gantt chart showing a schedule for designing, developing, purchasing, and installing a management information system.

Most projects, particularly long and complex ones, require several different schedules. For instance, the project manager will always want to have a master schedule to show the major tasks and the overall beginning and ending dates. In addition, there may be a requirement for additional schedules that show special events—for instance, tests. A common use of the Gantt chart is to show scheduled meetings or report due dates. Sometimes the project is so complex that several Gantt charts are needed to show the project detail.

Estimating Task Costs and Developing a Project Budget

The task costs are determined in the same way that the task durations are determined: The project team members talk to the individuals who will be doing the work. These individuals will have a good sense of how much the task will cost to accomplish. If, for instance, the task requires labor only and no equipment or materials, then the cost for it will be the labor rate of the individual(s) doing the task times the number of hours required to do the task.

Once the individual tasks have a cost against them, then it is an easy matter to aggregate the costs of all tasks under major WBS headings and finally for the total project.

Whether determining a project budget is really required is a matter of some controversy. Some argue that this is a waste of time when the budget is dictated by the organization. Clearly, this step is necessary when the planning is being done in preparation for submitting a bid for a contract to do a project. In that case, the budget development determines the cost and is the basis for the bid price. But what about when the project manager

Exhibit 11-2. Typical Gantt chart.

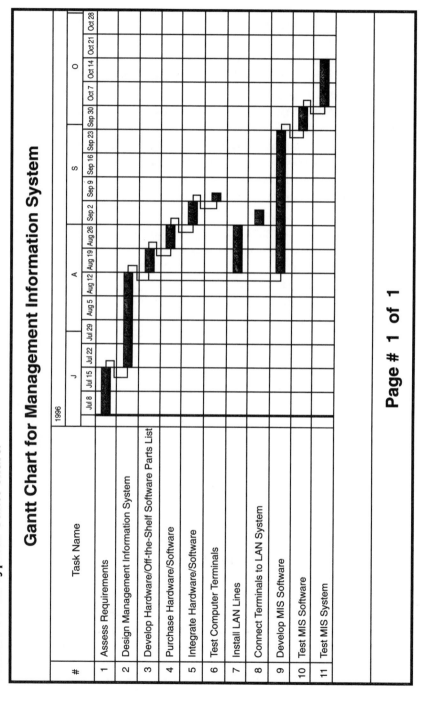

Gantt Chart for Management Information System

#	Task Name	1996																
			J				A				S					O		
		Jul 8	Jul 15	Jul 22	Jul 29	Aug 5	Aug 12	Aug 19	Aug 26	Sep 2	Sep 9	Sep 16	Sep 23	Sep 30	Oct 7	Oct 14	Oct 21	Oct 28
1	Assess Requirements																	
2	Design Management Information System																	
3	Develop Hardware/Off-the-Shelf Software Parts List																	
4	Purchase Hardware/Software																	
5	Integrate Hardware/Software																	
6	Test Computer Terminals																	
7	Install LAN Lines																	
8	Connect Terminals to LAN System																	
9	Develop MIS Software																	
10	Test MIS Software																	
11	Test MIS System																	

Page # 1 of 1

is given the project and told what the budget is? Is there any reason why she should redetermine the budget? The answer is a resounding yes!

When a project manager is handed a budget to do a project, the budget is usually a result of either a top-level estimate developed when the project was in the very early stage of conceptualization or the result of a contract won through a competitive bid. Either way, the chances are that the budget is not realistic.

Consider the case of the contract from a competitive bid. The contract was probably awarded because the organization had the lowest bid—too often far less than it really takes to do the work. Not only that, but senior management always reduces the contract price by the profit amount and often reduces it further to provide a reserve. In either case, the project manager is almost always starting the project with, at best, a very tight budget, or, at worse, a completely unachievable one. Therefore, the project manager has to develop an accurate budget in order to know at the beginning whether there are likely to be any budget problems. It is possible to accomplish the project within budget by reassessing the skill requirements, type and quality of equipment and materials, and numbers of personnel needed to do the job. However, this replanning can be achieved only if the amount of the potential shortfall is known.

Determining Final Resource Requirements

The project team will have determined, with a high degree of accuracy, the resource requirements for the project. However, it is only after the WBS is fully developed and each task and each subtask is identified that the team will really know what resources are going to be required. Once this is done, the project manager can adjust the team membership if required.

It is also at this time that the project manager can assign specific duties to the team members because the tasks can be completely identified and defined. A tool that helps in assigning these tasks and helps the project manager track and control the project is a task responsibility matrix, shown in Exhibit 11-3. This matrix is designed to show who is responsible for accomp-

Exhibit 11-3. Task responsibility matrix.

WBS Number	WBS Description	Task Duration	Primary Person Responsible	Secondary Person Responsible

lishing the work of each task in the WBS. In addition, it usually shows how long the task will take, and it can also show the budget assigned to the task. This matrix becomes particularly helpful when the budget, actual expenditures, and the earned value numbers are collected for project tracking.

The Project Plan Format

Exhibit 11-4 is a generic format for a project plan. With this format, a project team can develop a plan that can be used to accomplish a project's goals and objectives. I refer to this format as generic because it has been developed over a number of years and represents the basic elements required in just about any project. Many organizations or customers have developed their own plan formats to accommodate special requirements of the project. Therefore, the wise project manager will determine, during the conceptual phase, whether there are special plan requirements or not. If not, the format of Exhibit 11-4 will serve most situations.

The Executive Summary

This section is always written last because it is only after all the details of the project are known that the project manager and team can summarize the project.

The executive summary, typically directed to senior management, provides a summary of the background, scope, and objectives of the project. It should also contain a brief overview

Exhibit 11-4. A generic project plan format.

I. Executive Summary

II. Project Requirements and Objectives

III. General Methodology or Technical Approach

IV. Contractual Requirements

V. Schedules

VI. Resource Requirements

    A. Equipment

    B. Materials

    C. People

VII. Potential Risks

VIII. Performance Evaluation

of how the project will be accomplished, identify the customers, and talk about any special problems expected in the project and how they will be handled. For instance, if the project is large enough or complex enough that team members and consultants are needed, then it should be discussed in general terms. Risks and strategies for risk mitigation should also be addressed.

The executive summary should be viewed as exactly that—a summary. It usually is relatively short, about two pages, but can be longer depending on the size and complexity of the project. It should be written as succinctly as possible so that readers can quickly read and digest it but still be able to talk about the project with authority.

Project Requirements and Objectives

This section goes into depth about what the project is all about. It clearly states exactly what the requirements of the project are, the objectives of the project, the scope (that is, how large the project is), how long it will take to accomplish, and how many and what type of end products, what the measure of success will be, and how the project goals mesh with the organization's goals. This section is very detailed and can be several pages long.

General Methodology or Technical Approach

This section provides a narrative description of how the project manager and team will accomplish the project's goals. It should describe both the management and the technical approaches to accomplishing the project. Precise details of how to manufacture a part or the steps in developing some software are not required, but the general processes of each step of the project should be described.

This section should also discuss the relationship of the project's technical approach to existing technologies. If it is anticipated that new and different technologies will be required, this section should discuss how they will be integrated into the project.

Contractual Requirements

This section describes any special contractual requirements relative to the project: special reporting or deliverable schedules, payment cycles, specific types and numbers of tests and product demonstrations, reporting formats, required meetings or project reviews, and place and time of final delivery of the product.

This section also documents any special contractual requirements on vendors or consultants to the organization.

If the project customer is internal to the organization and there are no vendors or consultants, this section is not needed.

Schedules

The schedule section of the project plan may be quite long, and the schedules themselves may have to be drawn on fold-out sheets to accommodate them. The best approach is to provide a summary of key schedule points within the body of the plan and to attach the schedules themselves as appendixes to the plan. In that way, the appendixes can be detached if necessary, eliminating the problem of reading fold-out sheets in the middle of the plan document.

There may be more than one schedule in any project. There can be as many as five or six schedules for even relatively short and uncomplicated projects. How many schedules to prepare is strictly a function of the customer requirements (sometimes a customer will dictate separate schedules for different events) or whether preparing additional schedules will clarify or simplify the project tracking. How many schedules is usually a judgment call by the project manager. The key is to prepare as many schedules as required to track the project requirements.

Resource Requirements

Resources include all the personnel, equipment, facilities, and materials needed to accomplish the requirements of the project. It is better to break out these different resources to track their costs. Personnel, for instance, represent pure labor costs; materials is a cost category of its own.

All resources needed for the project are tabulated here. There are several reasons that a detailed accounting of all resources is important in the project plan. First, it is the only way truly to identify the project cost. Second, it provides the project manager with the leverage to negotiate for the needed resources. Third, once the project cost is determined, if the budget is less than the costs, the project manager and team can determine where cost reductions might be made by reassessing the project requirements against the identified resources.

Potential Risks

This is one of the most important sections of the project plan. It is the responsibility of the project manager and team to identify as many potential problem areas or risks as possible. The project sponsor or customer is also responsible for identifying any known risks. The reason is simple: It is far better to plan for a problem than to be surprised by it and have to work around it.

There are generally three types of risks: knowns, known unknowns, and unknown unknowns. A *known risk* is one that the project manager knows could happen and the impact is known—for example, some data are needed from one project before the second project can begin. If the schedule is so tight between the two that any delay in the first project would cause a delay in the second, then this is a known risk. A *known unknown* type of risk is one in which the project manager knows something will go wrong but doesn't know what the impact will be. For instance, we know that we will be receiving a telephone bill but don't know what the charges will be. An *unknown unknown* is one in which it is not known what will happen nor is it known what the impact will be.

Clearly, the project manager cannot anticipate every problem. However, using historical data and the experience of the team members, the project manager can identify and plan for much of the risk. For risks that cannot be anticipated, management reserves or other contingency plans can be developed.

Performance Evaluation

The last part of the plan format is the performance evaluation section. It is absolutely crucial for the project team to determine how the work of the project will be measured and the performance evaluated. Otherwise, how will the project manager know if the requirements of the project are being met?

Often projects have associated with them standards that are required by the customer, government regulating agencies, or other coding organizations. If that is the case, the evaluation procedures may be straightforward and clear. However, if there are no such existing standards, then the project manager and the project team must determine how they are going to assess the project's progress and what kind of "goodness" measure they will use. This evaluation strategy will have to be acceptable to the customer, and the project plan is an ideal way to communicate the strategy to all the stakeholders, including the customer.

Reviewing the Project Plan With the Customer

Finally, the project plan has to be reviewed with the customer regardless of whether the customer is internal or external to the organization. If the project is the result of winning a competitive bid, the project plan is part of the proposal that the organization has to submit in response to the customer's Request for Proposal. When the winner of a competitive bid is selected and the contract is awarded, the winner's proposal becomes part of the contract. In this case, the project plan has been reviewed and approved by the customer. In the case of an internal customer, however, it becomes the responsibility of the project manager to schedule time with the appropriate customer representatives to review and explain the project plan.

The need to review the project plan at this stage is simple: The next step is to implement the project and begin work. This is the last time the customer will have to review the project prior to starting work. It is also the last time, prior to starting work, that the project manager will have to ensure that the project team has correctly captured the customer's intent and accurately interpreted the project objectives and requirements.

Summary

The development or planning phase of the project is where the project is operationalized. All the analyses come together in a plan that allows the project manager to monitor and control the project to a successful conclusion. Some of the major tools used in the analyses of this phase are the:

- WBS
- PERT or precedence diagram
- Gantt charts
- Task responsibility matrix
- Project plan format

One of the key responsibilities of the project manager during this phase is to review the project plan with the customer. This review is the last action taken in this phase and is the final step toward implementing the project. Therefore, the review is the last opportunity for the customer to ensure that the project is going in the desired direction, and it is the last opportunity for the project manager to ensure that her interpretation of the project's objectives and requirements is the same as the customer's.

Once the project plan has final approval, the project can be implemented.

Chapter 12

The Implementation Phase

Hold fast the time! Guard it, watch over it, every hour, every minute! Unregarded it slips away, like a lizard, smooth, slippery, faithless, a pixy wife.

—Thomas Mann

The term *implementation phase* may be a little misleading because it implies simply putting something into motion. The implementation phase is indeed that, but it is much, much more. It is often called the main phase of the project—the phase during which the actual work is performed. Consequently, this is the phase in which the project is started, monitored, and controlled.

Project implementation is the process of putting the project plan into action. The plan is the road map of how the project should progress; the implementation phase is where the plan is turned into reality.

Monitoring is the process of assessing project performance or how the project is doing against what was planned. Very quickly it will become apparent to the project manager and team just how well they have planned the project when they start measuring actual against estimated performance.

Project control is the process of controlling the deviations from the plan. During the planning phase, such key things as the project budget and schedule are determined. Controlling the project's progress means controlling how closely the actual expenditures and work accomplished adhere to the plan.

Implementing the Project

Once a project is approved and given the go-ahead, the project manager's next step is to put those things in motion required to start performing the work of the project. This process is not an easy one. There are several steps that the project manager and the parent organization must go through in order to ensure that the project gets started on the right foot and moves according to the plan. Exhibit 12-1 shows the key steps in this process. These steps are planned during the development phase, but obviously cannot be acted on until the project manager and team receive the final approval to proceed. Note that many of the steps in Exhibit 12-1 are not sequential; they can be started in parallel. The primary consideration at this stage is to get the project underway as soon as possible while ensuring that each of the critical steps is accomplished.

Setting Up Cost Accounts

On small projects, it is generally not too difficult to monitor and control the project from one simple budget. The budget is used to track the project as a whole, and usually there is no compelling requirement to track the budget in greater detail than, say, the third level of the WBS. In larger, more complex projects, this approach would not have enough sensitivity to the nuances that

Exhibit 12-1. Steps in implementing a project.

- Set up cost accounts.
- Refurbish/rent/buy facilities.
- Collocate team.
- Design a monitoring system.
- Issue work orders.
- Contract with vendors.
- Issue Requests for Proposal for competitive bids.
- Hire personnel.
- Train personnel.

occur in multiple tasks or subtasks. Consquently, tracking the project variances would be impossible. Specifically, project overruns could be detected but not the source of the overrun.

To overcome this problem, the concept of *cost accounts* was developed: breaking the project down into smaller elements and monitoring each of these elements individually. Each element has its own cost or budget associated with it so that its progress can be measured directly against the planned budget.

In Chapter 5, we discussed the WBS and the work package in detail. The work package and the cost account are essentially the same. The workshop package is described by a WBS Dictionary. The term *dictionary* is used because it defines exactly what and how the work will be accomplished. The WBS Dictionary for each work package provides the following information:

- A short but concise description of the work to be accomplished
- A schedule to begin and finish the work
- Who, by name, is responsible for accomplishing the work
- A list of labor resources, materials, and equipment needed to accomplish the task
- A budget for the task

All of these characteristics of the work package are elements of the cost account with the exception that, in a cost account, the budget has to be time-phased to be monitored. The budget for each individual task can be time-phased on a Gantt chart or on one of the spreadsheets, such as Lotus 1-2-3 or Microsoft Excel, allowing a day-by-day assessment of expenditures against the plan.

Refurbish/Rent/Buy Facilities

Project managers usually do not have to be concerned with preparing or buying new facilities, but it does happen. Some projects require special work spaces or specialized tools, test equipment, or environmentally controlled work spaces. Under any of these circumstances, the project manager may find herself running a construction or refurbishment project before the primary project can begin.

Collocate the Project Team

It is strongly recommended that the project team be collocated if at all possible. This does not mean that the team has to be in the same large room, but all the members should be on the same floor of the building and, ideally, in the same general section on the floor.

There are several reasons that collocating the team is beneficial:

- It enhances good communication between the project manager and the team and among the team members.
- Working closely together on a project builds team spirit.
- Team morale is enhanced when team members feel that they are physically and mentally connected.
- Project problems often can be avoided when team members are close enough to discuss difficulties as they occur.

Although the ideal situation is for the team to be collocated, the reality is that most organizations do not have the space to collocate each project team. The next best alternative is to establish a "war room" for the team: a room set aside for the exclusive use of the project team. This is a large enough room for team meetings and for maintaining files relevant to the project.

Design a Monitoring System

Setting up a monitoring system is crucial to the control process. Without a way to track and analyze each of the tasks of a project, it is not possible to make the decisions necessary to control the project's progress.

Issue Work Orders

In order for the project to begin, the project manager must issue the appropriate work orders. In addition to authorizing the work to begin, each work order is a small but crucial part of the control process also. The work order specifies how requirements are to be fulfilled, how much can be spent on the task, and how long the work should take. John Nicholas, professor of engineering management at Loyola University, lists the following minimum information that is a part of every work order:[1]

- Statement of work
- Time-phased budget of direct labor hours, materials, and other direct costs
- Schedules, milestones, and relationships to other work packages
- Position of the task in the WBS
- Specifications and requirements
- Cost account number and position in the cost account structure
- Signatures of person authorizing and person accepting responsibility

Contract With Vendors

There are very few projects that do not have some vendor-required items. Although most organizations have a procurement department that specializes in contracting with vendors, it remains the project manager's responsibility to initiate the request for purchase. It is also the project manager, or the designated technical representative, who provides the requisite specifications for the requested item. In some cases, though, in particular when the technical solution requires the services of a team member rather than the services of a vendor, the project manager is responsible for negotiating the teaming agreement.

Issue Request for Proposal for Competitive Bids

The Request for Proposal (RFP) formally invites contractors or vendors to bid on some part of a project. For instance, your project might require a specialized software program that your company cannot develop. You would then prepare an RFP describing your project's requirement and a detailed specification that qualified companies could bid on. RFPs are issued with very precise instructions about how, where, and when bidders should respond. The response to the RFP is a proposal that contains, at a minimum, price and schedule estimates. A proposal also can contain a description of the responder's company, how they manage their tasks, risks associated with task development, and so on, depending upon what is specified in the RFP.

For most projects, RFPs to vendors or other contractors are simple, one- to five-page documents. Even so, the tendency is to bypass the formal RFP process, and simply call a favored supplier. Resist the urge to bypass the RFP process because issuing a formal RFP, if only in letter form, provides an audit trail, and it will reduce project costs through competition.

Hire Personnel

In many projects, the organizational strategy is to hire personnel to fill the specialized billets in the project organization. Although the human resources department is responsible for advertising for new employees and administering the hiring procedures, the project manager generally has the final decision on who is hired for the project. Hence, the project manager has to have a good understanding of interviewing techniques and procedures, as well as a thorough knowledge of the administrative processes, company benefits, and career potential with the organization.

Train Personnel

There may be a requirement to train some project members before they can begin work on the project. For instance, if the project is to develop specialized software using the customer's processes, procedures, or computer language, it may be necessary for the project manager to develop and schedule some special training courses. Or it may be that the parent organization possesses a cadre of trained personnel but not enough for the project. In any event, the project manager is responsible for ensuring the project team is prepared to accomplish the project's goals and objectives, and that often means a requirement for special training.

Monitoring the Project

Three activities make up the monitoring process: data collection, data analysis, and information reporting. The project manager's responsibility is to establish a process for collecting the data— how the information will be collected and how often— and set up a reporting hierarchy for disseminating the information after it is analyzed. To a very large degree, the reporting hierarchy will already be set as a part of the stakeholder analysis done in the conceptual phase. However, once the project gets underway, people who have not previously shown any interest in the project emerge. A good way to ensure that the reporting hierarchy is correct and is approved is to prepare a reporting matrix like the one in Exhibit 12-2. The wise project manager will then dis-

Exhibit 12-2. Sample reporting matrix.

Data Item	Report Description	Project Manager	Senior Management	Director of Engineering	Director of Software Development	Director of Contracts	Director of Finance	Customer Project Manager	
1	Status reports (monthly)	x	x	x	x	x		x	
2	Status reports (weekly)	x							
3	Monthly financial reports	x	x				x		
4	Configuration change reports	x		x	x				
5	Manpower utilization reports	x		x	x				
6	Exception reports	x	x						
7	Variance reports	x	x				x	x	
8									
9									
10									

tribute the proposed data distribution format with a memorandum asking for suggested additions and deletions to the reporting chain.

Data Collection

Sources of data are varied, and the project manager must take advantage of every one of them. The average project manager will spend approximately 90 percent of her time communicating with the project team, senior management, the customer, and other stakeholders. The majority of this time is spent either collecting or transmitting data.

Sources for data collection include:

- Project status meetings
- Individual task leader reports
- Employee time sheets
- Vendor and consultant invoices
- Telephone calls
- E-mail
- Management by walking around

Data collection does not have to follow a formal process. In fact, most project data are gathered informally. However, data going out of the project office are most often presented formally through a status report or status briefing.

Data Analysis

Collecting data is only half of the challenge; analyzing the material is the second half. We all know what it is like to experience information overload. Because the project manager spends so much time communicating with the project team, it is often the case that she is provided with so much information that it is not possible to process it all. The project manager quickly learns to distinguish between meaningful and useless data. But to do so requires close attention to detail and the ability to interpret the raw information.

Analyzing the data is a necessary step in the process because the data alone do not show what their impact is on the project. Before any information is processed out of the project team, there has to be an accurate assessment of the impact and a proposed solution for correcting any problems that might exist.

Most project data of concern involve the budget, the schedule, or the performance or quality of the project. Among the tools for analyzing the data relative to these three project characteristics, earned value is being used more and more for analyzing budget and schedule impacts. (Refer to Chapter 7 for a detailed discussion of earned value and how to apply it.)

Many organizations, though, still use a plot of budget against actual expenditures and estimated schedule against actual schedule to analyze progress. An example is shown in Exhibit 12-3 depicting the status of a project's actual expenditures against the budget at the three-month milestone.

The problem with this approach is that the project appears

Exhibit 12-3. Project budgeted against actual expenditures.

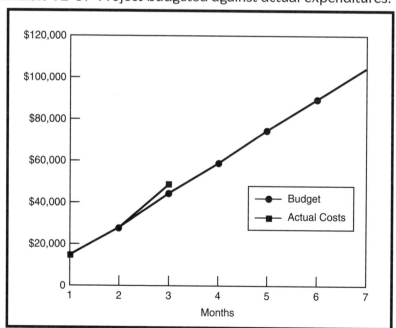

to be over budget but in actuality it may not be. It is not possible to tell from the information available. Suppose, for example, that the project plan called for buying several computers at month 4, but the vendor called to say that she was moving her store to larger quarters and wanted to reduce the size of her inventory significantly before the move. If she offered a reduced price to purchase the computers early, then the actual expenditures would show a marked increase at month 3, but in fact the project would not be over budget. With everything else being equal, the project would actually be under budget. It was precisely this kind of problem that led to the development of the earned value method for accounting for such changes in the project's schedule and accurately showing the status of the project.

Another way of analyzing the impact of data on a project is to use a variance worksheet. An example of one is shown in Exhibit 12-4. The variance worksheet is a good tool because it shows the variance in both the budget and the schedule and, consequently, would suggest that a change in one has a relationship to the other. Unfortunately, budget and schedule are not explicitly related on the variance worksheet as they are in the earned value analysis. Therefore, some interpretation is required.

A common use of the variance worksheet is in status reports. Senior managers do not have the time to read long reports, and a variance worksheet provides a lot of information quickly about the project's progress.

Information Reporting

Information reporting is done through either formal reports, such as status reports, or informational briefings.

The project manager or project team uses several different types of reports. All of these reports can be classified as status reports in a broad sense, but generally we use the term *status report* to refer to those that routinely describe the project's progress. Other types of reports detail problems or provide specialized information such as financial deviations or changes to the project baseline.

Exhibit 12-4. Variance worksheet.

Project Steps	Costs (dollars)				Schedule (days/weeks/months)			
	Budget	Actual	Variance	Total	Planned	Actual	Variance	Total

Status Reports

A status report is a narrative description of the project's progress, usually provided to senior management and the customer representative on a regular basis, say, each month. The frequency of the report, or any other report, usually is a function of how complex or risky the project is. For instance, a project involving new technology with significant financial consequences for the contractor or the customer would likely require frequent, informal status reporting—even daily—and formal reports due weekly or biweekly.

The type of information required on a status report varies from organization to organization. The basic information is shown in Exhibit 12-5. Some organizations opt for more detailed status reports rather than having several different reports for specialized reasons.

Variance Reports

Variances are deviations from the planned budget or schedule. Many customers, particularly external customers, require variance reports. The typical variance report will have a line graph showing the cumulative budget and schedule plotted against the actual budget and schedule. Any variances—positive if below budget or ahead of schedule and negative if over budget and behind schedule—have to be explained. If the project is over budget or behind schedule, the variance report will also have to reflect the plans to correct the problems.

Exception Reports

Exception reporting is a part of *exception management:* a way for senior managers to involve themselves in a project when something out of the ordinary happens. For instance, the project manager's functional supervisor, or another senior executive, may impose some limit on a key project element, usually budget, above or below which she has to be informed. An example might be that as long as actual expenditures are within, say, 10 percent of the budget, the project manager is responsible for cor-

Exhibit 12-5. Sample status report.

STATUS REPORT

Project Name: Report Date:

Project Phase: Report Period:

Project Manager:

Summary of Progress for Period:

Problems Encountered and Action Taken:

Planned Activities for Next Reporting Period:

Anticipated Problems:

Recommendations:

---

recting the variances. If the budget should exceed the 10 percent limit, above or below, then the project manager is obliged to issue an exception report to the appropriate manager for action.

Incidentally, we automatically assume that below budget or ahead of schedule is a good thing. However, the wise project manager will look with a jaundiced eye at a significant below-budget or ahead-of-schedule reading. Why? Being significantly below budget or ahead of schedule might indicate that all the required work on a task is not being accomplished.

Controlling the Project

To control a project generally means controlling four things:

1. Cost variances
2. Schedule variances
3. Scope changes
4. Risk

Cost Variances

Cost variances are deviations of actual expenditures from the project budget. Variances occur in every project because it is virtually impossible to predict with 100 percent accuracy what will happen once the project is underway. But controlling these deviations from the budget is a major problem in most projects.

The primary reason that budgets are overrun is that the project started with an unreasonable or underestimated budget. We have all heard or read about the horrendous budget overruns that often occur in DOD contracts. For those who are not familiar with the DOD process, the tendency is to assume the problem of overruns is caused by greedy contractors. Although some of these overruns may be the result of crafty contractors' working the system to their benefit, the simple fact is that cost overruns are usually the result of shaving the project costs too much in order to be the lowest bidder in a competitive environment. In every Request for Proposal (RFP) issued by the DOD is a statement to potential contractors declaring that the government has the right to award the contract on other than a cost basis. The RFP usually goes further and states that the contract will be awarded on the basis of *best value:* The highest bidder could win the contract if the government determines that, in the long run, the product from that contractor would be of greater value to the government than any of the other proposed solutions. For instance, one contractor's product might cost significantly more initially than another but cost far less to maintain over the product's lifetime. The best value in this case would be for the government to spend more initially to get the product whose lifetime or life cycle costs are less. Unfortunately, the government's acquisition process is administered in such a way that by the end of the proposal evaluation cycle, all the competitors will have had their proposals technically leveled; that is, all the competitors will have essentially equal technical solutions, and so the only discriminator left is price. Hence, "best value" then becomes the lowest price. All too often the winner will have lowered the bid price so much that the project cannot be accomplished for the contracted amount.

Of course, the lowest bid does not necessarily mean there will be a cost overrun. It certainly is possible to be the low bidder and still have a budget sufficient to accomplish the project's goals and objectives. However, what are the consequences of a too-low bid or one that "buys in"? We have already talked about the cost overruns and, perhaps, convincing the customer to pay for these overruns. Without a renegotiated contract, the only other options for the contractor are to *default*—that is, have the contract terminated because of the inability to perform—or to perform the contract within the budget provided but at a significantly reduced standard of quality.

The relevance of all this for the average project manager is that whether bidding on a contract or issuing RFPs to prospective vendors, the project manager must be sensitive to the problem of bids that are too low. Inevitably there will be cost overruns or products and services that fall far below the expected quality level.

Low bids are not the only reason for cost overruns. A major problem in many companies is the lack of any budget estimating system or, if there is one, an inaccuerate system. There are three categories of estimating methods:

1. *Order of magnitude estimate.* The order of magnitude estimate is simply a best guess. This type of estimate is usually done to get a ballpark number—a sense of the financial size of a potential project. This type of estimate is made with little or no data to support it. It is based purely on the person's experience and knowledge of the cost to accomplish generally similar projects. The accuracy of this type of estimate falls between −25 percent and +75 percent.

2. *Budget estimate.* The budget estimate is more accurate than the order-of-magnitude type: approximately −10 percent to +25 percent. An example of the budget estimate is the top-down estimate: The estimate is performed by senior management who draw on historical data relative to similar projects. This type of estimating considers major tasks or subcomponents of the project and is usually accomplished early in the project's life. The top-down method is not a bad estimating method, particularly when done by very experienced people who can draw on a good historical base. But it should be used to aid in the conceptual phase and be refined by a definitive estimate in the development or planning phase.

3. *The definitive estimate.* The bottom-up estimate is an example of a definitive estimate. *Bottom-up* means the estimating process is started at the lowest level of the WBS and aggregated upward to account for every element of the project. This is the most accurate method of the three types. It is accurate to within −5 percent to +10 percent and is done after the WBS has been fully developed.

Notice that in every case, the accuracy ranges of the estimating types are biased toward the positive side of the accuracy ranges. In other words, for the order-of-magnitude type, the mean of the accuracy range is 50 percent, for the budget estimate the mean is 15 percent, and for the definitive, it is 7.5 percent. This means that even with very accurate estimates, the tendency is to underestimate the cost of the project. Hence, the risk of a cost overrun is always present, and cost variances have to be monitored closely and managed tightly.

Schedule Variances

Schedule variances occur usually because of unreasonable schedule constraints. Generally the project team can estimate the actual duration requirements with reasonable accuracy, and if not, the PERT method provides a means for determining a reasonable task duration. The problem is not so much an inability to estimate the schedule but rather the imposition of a schecule that is too tight.

Most projects are initiated to meet specific needs, such as critical training, the improvement of existing systems, or competitive challenges. In most cases, these projects are reactive responses to a requirement and therefore start later than they should. If the projects are responding to critical needs, then there is always a sense of urgency, causing the completion date to be set unreasonably early. The late start and early completion create a compressed schedule that is almost never achievable.

If the cost or schedule variances become too large, the project plan will have to be rewritten, the schedule revised, or the end-item product redesigned.

Scope Changes

Changes to the project baseline are inevitable. They are caused by several different factors, including inaccurate budget and schedule estimates; government health, safety, or environmental standards mandates; and customer or project team recommended changes as project knowledge grows.

Change in a project is controlled through a *configuration management process*, a formal process designed by the project manager and team, or in some cases, an in-place organizational process, to screen recommended changes, track approved changes, and update the development process.

1. *Screening recommended changes.* Changes to a project can come from the customer as well as from team members and

other functional groups. These recommendations should be directed to the project manager, who will assess the impacts of the changes to the project. Many organizations have a change control board (CCB) concept to deal with this kind of change. CCBs are routinely found in engineering organizations where project changes have significant technical impact. Membership on a CCB consists of three to five persons representative of the company's technical expertise. CCB meetings are usually scheduled or called rather regularly, since project changes require quick decisions, and waiting for the next CCB meeting could affect the project schedule. If a CCB does not exist, the project manager should form one because every project, especially complex ones, will have a large number of requests that need to be handled expeditiously. Some of the requested changes will have no effect on the project budget, schedule, or resources, and the project manager usually is authorized to approve these changes unilaterally. However, if there is an impact on the project, the changes should be approved only by higher authority or a CCB.

2. *Tracking approved changes.* Once a change is approved, the project manager's designated configuration management specialist must document the changes and update the project specifications. In large contracts, the configuration management process is very elaborate and very detailed, with each change documented, numbered with a configuration item number, and logged. The configuration management position is so important that it has become a separate labor category and is considered to be a specialist function.

3. *Updating the development process.* After the change is approved and the files are updated, the project baseline is updated, the changes are published, and all stakeholders are informed of the changes. Changes to the baseline often—in fact usually—require a change to the contract. No project changes should ever be approved without an attendant change to the contract. Even if the customer decides to change the baseline configuration and it is determined that there is no impact on the budget or schedule, a no-cost contract modification should be requested by the project manager. Usually the customer will automatically issue one, but the experienced project manager will always insist on

having the modification prior to instituting the changes. These contract modifications are necessary because one of the actions at project completion is to determine whether the goals, objectives, and specifications have been met. Without a constract modification, there is no way to track whether or why a change was made.

Risk

As defined by the Project Management Institute, project risk management "includes the processes concerned with identifying, analyzing, and responding to project risk. It includes maximizing the results or positive events and minimizing the consequences of adverse events."[2] PMI further states that risk management is made up of four major processes:

- Risk identification
- Risk quantification
- Risk response development
- Risk response control

The risk management cycle is depicted in Exhibit 12-6.

Risk Identification

Risk identification should be an ongoing preoccupation of the entire project team. We have already examined the importance of identifying potential problem and risk areas. Clearly, it is not possible to anticipate all problems, but as the project is defined and the project team gains a better understanding of the requirements, the risk areas will become clearer. Among the sources of information to aid in the identification of risks, three are the most common:

1. *Project specifications.* The project specifications are the first best source of information about the project and the potential risk areas. Specifications describe the project in detail. They provide constraints such as budget and schedule, and sometimes other constraints, such as specific technological, materials,

Exhibit 12-6. Risk management cycle.

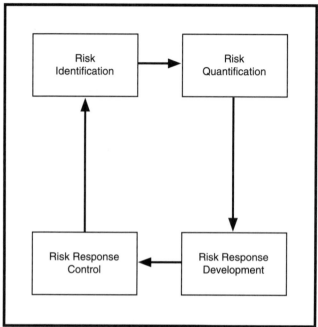

or size and weight requirements, all of which may constitute risk areas. While the specifications are being developed or interpreted, the project team should note all risk areas.

2. *Project management plan.* Most of the risk areas will be identified during the development of the project management plan. The reason is that the tools for developing the plan—WBS, network analysis, Gantt charts—contribute to the microscopic examination of the project and all its components. Consequently, many risk areas, particularly those related to budget, schedule, and resource allocation, will be identified.

3. *Historical data.* Documenting the lessons learned in every project will pay dividends when they are reviewed for problem areas. Experienced project managers often create databases dedicated to the risks encountered in previous projects and how they were resolved. It is far better to learn from someone else's mistakes than from your own.

Some of the tools that are very useful in identifying risks are:

- Flowcharting
- Brainstorming
- Checklists
- Cause-and-effect diagrams
- Interviewing
- Lessons-learned documentation

Risk Quantification

Risk quantification means determining the potential impact of the risk to the project. Quantifying the risks will enable the project manager to determine whether to accept the risk, pass it off to someone else, or avoid it altogether.

Among the tools that can be used to quantify risk are statistical methods, which provide the project manager with probabilities of the event's happening; simulations, which will show whether the event is likely to happen and the result if it does; and decision trees, to determine whether the risk is worth taking. Sometimes risks are quantified by hiring experts in the field to assess the risk event and determine the probability and the impact. All of these tools are used to generate data from which a response to the risks can be made.

Risk Response Development

Once the risks are identified and the impacts to the project are determined, the project team has to decide the most advisable approach toward each risk event.

Some risks are worth taking because of the potential payoff to the project. For instance, a particular piece of high-technology equipment or a special computer chip might be in the early stages of use, but the project would benefit significantly from the use of these items. If the items work as planned, then the project reaps substantial benefits. If the items do not work as planned, the entire project may have to be redone from scratch. This is a big risk, but it might be well worth accepting it.

Some risks have to be faced, but the project manager might prefer to pass that risk to someone else—perhaps a vendor or a teammate. A common risk that occurs in nearly every large project is associated with marginal capability in one or more of the requirement areas of the project. For instance, company A may have strong capabilities in all aspects of a large program except in computer-based training deveopment. If the project requires some computer-based training programs, then the company A project manager might want to consider teaming with company B, which specializes in computer-based training. That way, company A's risk of not being able to fulfill the computer-based training component of the contract is passed on to company B, and the team of A and B would consider that the computer-based training development component is not a risk item.

Risk Response Control

The next step in the risk management process is to develop a risk management plan that deals with the identified risk events and provides guidance for the unidentified risks.

The risk management plan outlines contingency plans for all the identified risks and provides guidance for work-around plans for unexpected risks.

It is important to remember that the risk identification, quantification, response development, and response control cycle continues throughout the project's life cycle. Even risks that are identified early may have more impact than originally thought, and, if so, will require that these risks be requantified and a new response control strategy implemented.

Contingency Plans and Work-Arounds

As a part of the risk management process, the project team will develop a *contingency plan:* a plan to handle a risk should it materialize. The plan will identify the risk, its impact on the project, what action has to be taken to mitigate the risk, and who is reponsible for the action.

Contingency plans also should be written to address unknown risks, that is, risks that cannot be identified but, from experience and history, probably will occur. Since the risk is an unknown, only a process can be identified for handling it should it occur. Many organizations have standard guidelines to handle such occurrences. One of the major characteristics of planning for unknown risks is the establishment of a *contingency fund*, a fund in place to ensure that the project does not suffer delays as a result of an unexpected risk event's happening. The amount set aside by the organization for contingencies is usually some predetermined percentage amount of the project. This percentage will have been determined from historical data—that is, an average of unexpected costs for all similar projects.

A *work-around* is an action or actions taken to handle the impact of an unexpected risk event. Work-arounds occur more often than any project manager would like because it is impossible to identify all risks. That is why it is so crucial for the project team to be constantly involved in the risk management cycle. Any warning of a risk event, even with a one-day notice, could save the project from costly schedule or budgetary losses.

Summary

The implementation phase of a project life cycle involves starting the project, monitoring its progress, and controlling day-to-day activities so that variances from the project plan are kept to a minimum.

The key to success in this phase is the monitoring system design. If the project manager and team put into place a systematic way to collect data, analyze the data, control the variances revealed in the analyses, and report the results quickly, the project will progress smoothly. Otherwise the project will be characterized by constant, reactive attempts to put out fires.

Another key aspect of project success revolves around the expertise and efficiency of the team in risk management. Amazingly, a very large segment of the corporate world does not engage in any formalized risk planning process. Not to do so is to invite disaster.

The key tools for this phase of the project are the WBS, Gantt charts, network analyses, earned value analyses, decision trees and statistical analyses, and various report formats.

Notes

1. John M. Nicholas, *Managing Business and Engineering Projects: Concepts and Implementation* (Englewood Cliffs, N.J.: Prentice Hall, 1990). Copyright © 1990. Reprinted by permission of Prentice-Hall, Inc., Upper Saddle River, N.J.
2. William R. Duncan, *A Guide to the Project Management Body of Knowledge* (South Darby, Penn.: PMI. 1996).

Chapter 13
The Termination Phase

Do not turn back when you are just at the goal.
—Publilius Syrus

One characteristic of a project is that it is of temporary duration. By definition, every project has an end. The problem is that projects have a definite ending point only if there is a formal ending to the project. Otherwise, they can extend beyond what would normally be considered the ending point, even for years beyond. In my seminars, I often have students who ask, "How do you get a project to end?" or, "I have a project that never seems to go away."

The termination phase is as important as any other phase, but many organizations don't support the activities of this phase because of the competitive pressure to start other projects even as the current project is winding down. Nevertheless, the project manager needs to focus on the termination phase with the same intensity as, or maybe more than, the other phases.

Terminating a project is one of the most important, and often one of the most difficult, phases of the project's life cycle. The problem is that when the project approaches the end, the team members begin looking for their next assignment, and they may lose interest in the project they are working on. Also, functional managers begin to siphon off team members, assigning them to other projects. The net result is that the project manager is often faced with the task of bringing the project to closure with virtually no resources.

To preclude some of the problems encountered during project closure, the project manager should begin planning for the termination phase at the beginning of the project. Project managers who focus on the one goal of delivering the end item to the customer are too narrow in their perspective and fail to define other, equally important goals—goals that should be part and parcel of every project in the organization. In Exhibit 13-1, I have listed the general goals of every project manager during the termination phase of a new project. Naturally, this list is not inclusive. Each project will have to be tailored to the organization's goals, and each project manager and team will also have several personal goals to strive for.

One can make the argument that the goals in Exhibit 13-1 are nothing more than what the project manager should be doing anyway as a part of the job, and that is absolutely correct. The problem is that not every project manager or organization will worry about anything much beyond items 1 and 2 unless they are adopted as formal goals of the project.

Why Projects End

Projects end for essentially three reasons:

1. The project goals and objectives are met.
2. The benefits or original reasons for the project no longer are viable.
3. The contractor defaults on the project.

Exhibit 13-1. The general project termination goals of every project manager.

1. Provide the customer with the product or service specified.
2. Strive to meet the project goals on time and on budget.
3. Maintain open communications with all stakeholders.
4. Request and support at least two audits during the project life cycle.
5. Document and file in the organization's library a complete history of the project.
6. Document lessons learned for the project.
7. Actively seek new positions for the project team members.

Clearly, the number one reason is the most desirable reason of them all. The objective always is to terminate the project after all the requirements are met and to do it in a planned, disciplined, and orderly fashion. The steps in achieving this planned, disciplined, and orderly termination will be discussed later in this chapter.

The second reason for termination is by far the most difficult one—difficult in terms of coming to grips with the necessity and advisability of terminating the project and then acting on it. (This is not the most damaging reason for termination, but it is the most difficult one.) These are the projects that had good goals and objectives and might even have been managed efficiently and effectively. There may not be anything inherently wrong with these projects except that they are no longer relevant to the organization's or customer's overall strategic or business goals. Project managers and their organizations don't like to terminate a project once it gets started and before it is completed. Perhaps they view such a termination as a failure, but rather than a failure, evaluating the efficacy of a project periodically and deciding whether it should continue is a sound business practice.

Every project, especially those for internal customers, should have go/no-go decision points to provide senior management with an opportunity to reassess the project as it reaches predetermined milestones and make a decision whether it is beneficial to continue.

Suppose senior management decides to pursue a new line of business, one significantly different from usual business endeavors. The project manager for this effort has been given a budget to modernize, change, or buy new equipment as appropriate, hire people with the requisite skills, and begin producing the product. However, because this new business line is so different, the planners underestimated the start-up costs. Now that the project is underway and the project team is more sophisticated about the real requirements and costs, the project manager can present the senior executives with a more realistic estimate of the costs for getting into this new market area.

The benefits may far outweigh the costs in this scenario, making it worth the additional expense to continue with the project. But suppose the senior managers discover that they may not be able to capitalize their investment. What should the company do? The answer seems patently clear: Cut the losses and terminate the project. Coming to that conclusion and making that decision can be excruciating, and many organizations continue to pour money into that hole before they can accept that it just does not make any sense to continue with the project.

Sometimes the customer makes the decision that the project should not continue. This decision, especially if from an external customer, can be devastating to the contractor. Even if the customer is happy with the work of the contractor, the perception often exists that the project was terminated because the contractor did not perform up to expectations. In addition, having the project terminated, even on good terms, means having a project team without assigned or billable work.

The third category for terminating a project is by far the worst. When a contractor defaults or the customer has to terminate for cause, that means the contractor did not perform technically—in short, it could not or did not produce. Being terminated because of the inability to perform technically damages the company's reputation and demoralizes employees.

Project Management Activities During the Termination Phase

The primary responsibility of the project manager is to ensure that all work on the project has been completed. But completing the project is only a small part of the work that has to be accomplished in this phase. Exhibit 13-2 provides a checklist of the major activities that have to be accomplished in the termination phase.

Activities With the Customer

If the project manager establishes a close working relationship with the customer, as should be the case, then getting to final closure on the end item will not be too difficult. Acceptance of

Exhibit 13-2. Project manager's checklist of termination activities.

---

1. Customer
   - Deliver end item.
   - Install and test end item.
   - Review project scope with customer.
   - Obtain formal acceptance from customer.
2. Project Organization
   - Recognize and reward project team members.
   - Reassign project personnel.
   - Provide personnel reports and recommendations to functional managers.
3. Financial
   - Submit final invoice to customer.
   - Submit final payments to vendors.
   - Close all project charge codes.
4. Site/Equipment
   - Close project site.
   - Dispose of equipment and furniture.

---

the end item by the customer should be virtually a formality if the project manager and customer have monitored the project closely, talked about and resolved any discrepancies as they occurred, and had agreement on the project goals and objectives in the first place.

One difficulty at this stage is in making sure that all the deliverables are turned over to the customer and all are accepted. For instance, most products, and sometimes services, require supporting documentation, such as operating or training manuals. Sometimes one of the deliverables will be a support plan or the initial stock of spare parts. The point is that the project manager has to view the project as a system and ensure that everything is accounted for.

Many projects often require installation and testing of end items delivered to the customer. It is not uncommon for the customer to withhold some percentage of the contract price, say 10 percent, until the installation, testing, and, occasionally, some

period of operation are completed. Only then, when the customer is completely satisfied that the product delivered is the
product contracted for, will the final payment be made and the
contract closed. All of these contractual requirements have to be
planned for at the beginning of the project so they can be dealt
with at project close-out.

Another difficulty in the termination phase is the amount
of paperwork required and the effort needed to ensure it is all
completed. We will discuss the different reports that have to be
accomplished as each of the major termination activities is addressed.

Organizational Activities

Project termination is usually an emotional time for the project
team. Sometimes it can be depressing. If team members have
been hired solely for that project, project termination can mean
that some team members will be laid off. But even without the
specter of a layoff, team members will be anxious about what
their next job is, causing disruption in the project.

One of the great ironies in project management is that if a
project manager gets complete team member buy-in at the front
end of the project, which is what we all strive for, it can backfire
as the project approaches termination. The reality is that if team
members become too attached to the project, they sometimes
will sabotage it to prevent it from ending—and at the very time
the project manager needs complete teamwork to close the project and make the schedule.

The termination phase is also the phase during which personality problems emerge as a major source of conflict.[1] This
really is not surprising since it is during this period that the
interesting project work is completed, and team members are
either being siphoned off for other projects or are worrying
about their new assignment—even whether there will be a new
assignment. The project manager has to be sensitive to these
problems and endeavor to keep the team focused on finishing
the requirements.

Although the project manager has no functional authority

over project personnel, he or she should make every reasonable effort to facilitate reassignment to other projects as each individual's work is finished. There are two reasons that trying to get team members reassigned should be a priority with the project manager: It is the right thing to do, and it will pay enormous dividends for both the project manager and the organization in the future.

Helping team members get reassigned after project termination is the right thing to do because they have, after all, dedicated themselves to the successful accomplishment of the project. Without the team and team member support, the project manager would never accomplish the project goals and objectives. And the best reward for any employee is a demonstration that the work is appreciated and valued. Finding new work for these employees in the organization is the highest form of flattery.

The second reason for helping team members find new assignments is a little self-serving but important nonetheless. Helping to find new jobs for the team reflects well on the project manager and the organization. The team members will respond with loyalty and support. The old unwritten contract between employee and employer—if an employee worked hard and was loyal to the company, he would have a job for life—no longer exists. That feeling of trust between employer and employee needs to be rebuilt, and helping the team member find a new job within the organization is a step in that direction.

One of the reports that the project manager will submit during termination is a personnel report. Since the project manager has no functional authority over team personnel, he is not the person to write performance reviews. However, the project manager is often asked to make comments for an individual's performance review because he will have observed the individual's work and team behavior at close hand. In the same vein, the project manager should submit a personnel report to all the appropriate functional managers, detailing each individual's work ethic, team skills, technical expertise, and whether the person should be assigned to future projects. This report should have limited and confidential distribution.

Financial Activities

Getting paid for the project work is a significant milestone in any project and is, of course, the reason the company is in business. But there are other financial matters that have to be attended to as well.

Almost every project will have vendors supporting it. The project manager has to ensure that all vendors are notified that the project is closing and that all outstanding invoices have been submitted. The project manager also has to close all charge codes used in the project, by notifying the accounting department and all functional groups in the company that no charges against the project will be accepted after a given date.

Site and Equipment Close-Out

Many projects are executed on-site, which means that the contractor performs on the project at the customer's location. Often the customer provides office or work space for the project, but usually "on-site" means that the contractor has to lease office and work space within a specified radius of the customer's location. If the project is accomplished on the customer's premises, there may not be much site-closing activity required beyond the removal of personal belongings and company equipment. In the latter case, the project manager will have to close out the lease, stop all utilities, disconnect telephone service, and notify all suppliers. In either case, the project manager is responsible for packing and shipping the company-owned supplies and equipment back to the parent company.

Often, particularly with government contracts, the customer will furnish equipment to the contractor to accomplish the job. For instance, it is common for a customer to furnish special test equipment or special tools to a project. It is also common for the customer to furnish computers to a project, particularly if the project is to develop some type of computer-based training. The customer provides the computers so that the software can be developed, loaded, and tested before shipment to the customer. In each case, the equipment provided for the project still belongs to the customer and must be accounted for and returned to the customer at the end of the contract. (A special case of customer-furnished equipment occurs when the customer has excess equipment or parts and provides them to the contractor as a cheaper alternative than manufacturing them anew.)

Auditing the Project

One of the final tasks of the project team is to perform a complete evaluation of the project. This task is often overlooked, but it is essential that every project, regardless of how the project ended, be evaluated for lessons learned. Unless there is a formal review, the tendency is to suppress problems encountered and understate the impact of past errors or misjudgments.[2] In short, we convince ourselves that things weren't really so bad after all.

Some authors refer to this stage as *evaluation* or *summary evaluation*. I prefer to call this an *audit* because "audit" implies a more disciplined approach, greater detail, and a look at every aspect of the project.

The problem with any evaluation of work done is a tendency to explain away or gloss over things that went wrong or point fingers and lay blame for problems. Project evaluations are not to fix blame but to review the performance of the team and the project end item. Making this evaluation a formal one tends to result in a more objective evaluation and with data that are more useful to the organization.

There should be a true audit of the project midway through the schedule as well as at the end, and these audits are best done by an independent team of experts as opposed to the project team. The reason for an independent audit team is, of course, to get around the problems I mentioned. An independent audit team can encounter other and quite different problems:

- Resentment by the project team
- Fear that the audit team will uncover problems (hence, the project team is not forthcoming with information)
- Disruption to the project

- Less understanding of the project's goals and objectives and thus biased conclusions
- Fear by the project team that the auditors will place blame for problems

The project manager has to be sensitive to these problems and work to mitigate the project team's fears and facilitate a quick and accurate audit. One way to do this is to include on the audit team people who are known and respected by the project team. It is not uncommon to request that a senior member of the project team be part of the audit process, a solution that offers two major benefits: It serves to calm the project team, and it is a way for the audit team to reach more accurate conclusions by having someone intimately familiar with the project to interpret the project goals, objectives, and requirements.

The audit team composition is critical to the success of the audit process. It is usually my recommendation that someone other than the project manager—perhaps the project manager's supervisor—organize the team. The size of the audit team is generally a function of the size of the project; a large, complex project requires a larger audit team to evaluate it. Audit team members can be drawn from a variety of areas, but all should have expertise in some aspect of the project. Some of the areas from which team members can be recruited are:

- Contracts
- Marketing
- Finance or accounting
- Human resources
- Technical functional groups
- Facilities
- Logistics

Whatever the makeup of the audit team, the members have to approach the evaluation with complete objectivity. It is their job to evaluate the performance of the project team, including the project manager, and the performance of the project.

The audit report contains an assessment of every aspect of

the project. Exhibit 13-3 is a format that can be used as a guide to writing the report. Clearly, not every project will require a format as complete as this one. Each project will have more or fewer elements than are represented in the exhibit. But in general, it is helpful to have a format available, and companies that support the audit process usually have a standard format as part of their operating procedures.

The project manager should also remember that the audit report is a communication tool. Therefore, it is her responsibility to prepare a distribution list for the document. Again, if the organization has a standard audit format, then it will likely have a minimum distribution list as well.

As a word of caution, there are two things that should never happen. First, the audit report should be prepared in a professional manner and never contain derogatory remarks about individuals. Any assessments of an individual's behavior or performance should be documented but should have limited and confidential distribution. Second, the project manager should never allow senior management to be blind-sided. If there are problems that the project manager knows will surface in an audit report, the appropriate senior management should be advised about them before reading them in the final audit report.

Summary

The termination phase of the project life cycle is as important as any other phase, yet many project managers and their organizations do not place as much value on this phase as it deserves. The primary reason is that any organization that is basically project oriented and, especially, dependent on external contracts for their core business is under enormous competitive pressure to move on to new projects as quickly as possible. This usually means that functional managers start reassigning project team members to new projects even before their old assignment is completed.

Exhibit 13-3. Example format for a final project audit report.

Project Audit Report for _____

I. Executive Summary
II. Introduction
III. Project Review
    A. Project objectives
    B. Methodology or approach
IV. Planning Effectiveness
V. Project Management Effectiveness
VI. Effectiveness of Technical Solution
VII. Project Deliverables
    A. Description
    B. Assessment against requirements
VIII. Quality
    A. Standards used
    B. Measuring
    C. Assessment against requirements
IX. Schedule
    A. Delays
        1. Reasons
        2. Recovery actions
    B. Assessment against plan
X. Finances
    A. Problems
        1. Reasons
        2. Recovery actions
    B. Assessment against plan
XI. Resources Utilization
    A. Effectiveness
    B. Problems
        1. Reasons
        2. Recovery actions
XII. Individual Team Member Assessment and Recommendations (submit as separate, confidential report)
XIII. Lessons Learned
XIV. Recommendations

The project manager must plan for the termination phase well in advance of the scheduled project end—ideally in the development phase of the project life cycle. And the project manager must resist, within realistic bounds, the siphoning off of team members prior to a formal project termination date. Although this is not easy to do since the project manager does not have functional authority over the team members, one thing that can help is to include the termination requirements and responsibilities in the project charter.

Although the primary emphasis in any project is to provide the end product to the customer on time and on schedule, the project manager must not forget that there are ancillary support items required in each project. For instance, almost every project requires documentation such as operating manuals. The project manager has to ensure that all requirements of the project are satisfied.

Finally, one important task in the termination phase that is often overlooked is the final audit or evaluation. This important task is critical to the organization because it is from these audits that future projects can be made better. The audit is accomplished principally for the lessons learned that can be applied to future projects.

Notes

1. H. J. Thamhain and D. L. Wilemon, "Conflict Management in Project Life Cycles," *Sloan Management Review* (Summer 1975).
2. John M. Nicholas, *Managing Business and Engineering Projects: Concepts and Implementation* (Englewood Cliffs, N.J.: Prentice Hall, 1990).

Index

acknowledging contributions/accomplishments, 71–73
activities on the arrows (AOA), 93–94, 98–99, 100*f*, 101–102, 102*f*, 104
activities on the nodes (AON), 93–94
actual cost of work performed (ACWP), 118
Air Force, U. S., 116
analytical hierarchy process (AHP), 140
auditing the project, 237–238, 239, 240*f*
authoritarian leadership, 62–63
average rate of return (ARR), 142–143

Bass, Bernard, on leadership, 61–62
behavioral skills, 16, 148
benefit-to-cost ratio (BCR), 143–146
body language, 22–23, 40
budgeted cost of work performed (BCWP), 120*f*, 120–122
budgeted cost of work scheduled (BCWS), 118
budget estimating, 219–220
Burnham, Daniel H., on plans, 183
business skills, 16, 148

career path, project management as a, 10–11
change control board (CCB), 222
charter, preparing project, 167–169, 168*f*
clarification, asking for, 40–41
collaboration, fostering, 69–70
collocate project team, 208
communication skills
  negotiation skills, 51
  persuading, 14
  potential channels of communication, 19–20

project manager as a communicator, 18–19
  sending and receiving messages, 20–23
  see also verbal communication
competence and leadership, 65
conceptual phase, 151, 152*f*
  charter, preparing project, 167–169, 168*f*
  core project team, 157–159
  initiating the project, 152–154
  opportunity and opportunity alternatives, assessing, 154–155
  plan, high-level project, 159–160, 161*f*, 162–167, 166*f*
  scope definition, 156
  sponsor of a project, 156–157
  summary, 169
configuration management process, 221
conflict in a project, 45–49
contingency plans, 226–227
contractual requirements, 201
controlling a project
  cost variances, 218–221
  risk, 223–227
  schedule variances, 221
  scope changes, 221–223
  work breakdown structure, 89
core project team
  collocate the, 208
  conceptual phase, 153–154, 157–159
  conflicts, 47
  development phase, 183–186
cost-effective companies, 5–6
cost of a project, 88, 165, 195, 197, 206–207
cost performance index (CPI), 123–124
cost schedule control system criteria (C/SCSC), 117